SECURITY NOTICE

The Soul of

FONDA SAN MIGUEL

Fifty Years of Food and Art

Bartender Jimmy Orchowski

This book is dedicated to Miguel Ravago, Diana Kennedy, and the many past and present esteemed employees, vendor partners, and guests who have contributed enormously over these fifty years.

May I simply say from the heart:
¡MUCHISMAS GRACIAS!

TOM GILLILAND

The Soul of

FONDA SAN MIGUEL

Fifty Years of Food and Art

By Tom Gilliland

Foreword by Aaron Franklin

CONTENTS

By Aaron Franklin

Foreword

Most people know me as the barbecue guy, but the reality is that I dabble in so many things—from Hot Luck, Food and Music Festival, our other restaurant, to the Uptown Sports Club; from books and shows to building custom stuff in the shop for all the above. The common denominator has always been food and my love for restaurants. It's no surprise that Fonda San Miguel is at the top of my list of favorite spots and a Franklin family staple. We eat there a lot. It's been in full weekly rotation for quite some time. And for good reason.

Fonda San Miguel is an iconic restaurant that always executes on a high level. You don't get to reach fifty years in the business by being anything less. I didn't have the honor of meeting Chef Miguel Ravago. In fact, when asked to write this forward, I had yet to meet Tom Gilliland, but that didn't matter. Fonda has always been an inspiration for how to run a restaurant that can be so many things to so many people and be such a well-grounded place in the community. I've eaten at Fonda hundreds of times. It always feels new and exciting, familiar and comforting, super casual and fancy at the same time. Truly a feat for any restaurant.

Fonda San Miguel is a North Star in the restaurant world. No one opens a restaurant with the goal of lasting a couple of years. No, you pour your heart and soul into it, constantly pivoting and always rolling with the punches, and it doesn't always work out as planned. I'm sure Fonda has ups and downs, but guests would never know it. It has always checked the two most critical boxes for a restaurant: consistency in excellent food and the most personal service. A third checked box is a bonus: being accessible to all, whether you want casual appetizers and drinks with friends for a quick happy hour or a perfect place for a long leisurely dinner to celebrate special occasions. I've been there for both and many in between.

As a guy who is knee deep into our own restaurants, I admit that I may be sensitive to recognizing another ingredient commonly used in successful restaurants. It is not usually accounted for and sometimes goes unnoticed for years. It's the magic. At Franklin Barbecue, we've been farming genetically unmodified hormone-free unicorns since the beginning. I'm not sure what Fonda does, but it's been working its own magic for fifty years and counting.

I grew up in Bryan, Texas, in two family businesses. My grandparents ran a music store that greatly influenced my love for local business and community, and my parents ran a small restaurant that made me appreciate all the moving parts and how many things must happen to make the dream work.

I got myself to Austin as soon as possible, landing here in the nineties as an optimistic teenager with a love for all things rock and roll and the goal of doing something that was uniquely me. I also arrived with almost no money at all. My love for food and a personal mission to find all the cool local spots led me to Fonda. I remember the coziness of the atrium. The stories told by the walls made me feel as though I was somewhere truly special. The scent of mole provided the comfort the soul needs; the energy and buzz of the dining room got me. I was hooked. I sat down, giddy with new adventure. I quickly ordered chips and salsa, and I took a sip of the finest water Austin's limestone aquifer had to offer. I looked at the menu, bound in rich leather, and politely asked for the check and got the heck out of there! Yeah, that darn money thing again.

Like everyone else in Austin, I played music for years, which led me to cross paths with this extraordinarily brilliant and funny person named Stacy. She's been my magic ever since. Together we opened Franklin Barbecue. We had hopes and dreams of one day being an iconic restaurant that's always been there, providing food that consistently comforts and inspires our guests in the same way we've been inspired by so many before us. We have been truly blown away by the support of Austin and the world around us. Like Fonda, we have no interest in not being the best we can be, and like Tom, we are always around to make sure everyone feels welcome and like part of the family.

Over the years we have become quite the regulars at Fonda, with our own family hitting the 5 o'clock happy hour in the atrium for our usual faves. I see our kiddo with a familiar wide-eyed love for restaurants and hospitality, and it thrills me to no end to share these meals and create these memories. Thank you, Fonda, for the years of impeccable service and delicious food. We look forward to many more, and we're really excited to welcome Tzintzuntzan to the mix.

Aaron Franklin, center, with his wife, Stacy, and daughter, Vivian.

Niña, *by Maria de Los Angeles Pedrosa. Tom bought the painting in 1977 for $3 while taking a walk in Sullivan Park off the Reforma. Is la niña laughing mischievously or hiding a sweet giggle? Either way, patrons see her when entering the atrium and most can't help but smile.*

Introduction

It Takes a Village!

FIFTY YEARS! What an adventure this has been! "It takes a village," and Fonda San Miguel has great inhabitants, too many to name. They know who they are and can take pride every day.

The challenge for any restaurant with iconic status and this longevity is to not become stagnant. Fonda San Miguel intends to continue innovating—while remaining authentic.

Because culinary Mexico is so diverse, it is possible to have many authentic restaurants. How the landscape has changed since we first opened, when even black beans (frijoles negros) weren't available.

Our mission from the beginning—Houston in 1972, Austin in 1975—continues to be to present our patrons with this extraordinary regional cuisine.

TOM GILLILAND
Co-founder and Owner of Fonda San Miguel

"Give me five eyes, four noses, and seven ears," instructed Tom, as he commissioned artist Roi James to paint his portrait. The artist complied by creating multiple exposures and a custom frame, featuring mini portraits of Tom's beloved dogs in each corner and a Superman symbol reflecting Tom's superpowers. It hangs in the main dining room opposite Miguel Ravago's portrait, also by Roi James, which was a surprise going-away gift Tom commissioned and presented to the late executive chef before he left on an extended visit to Europe.

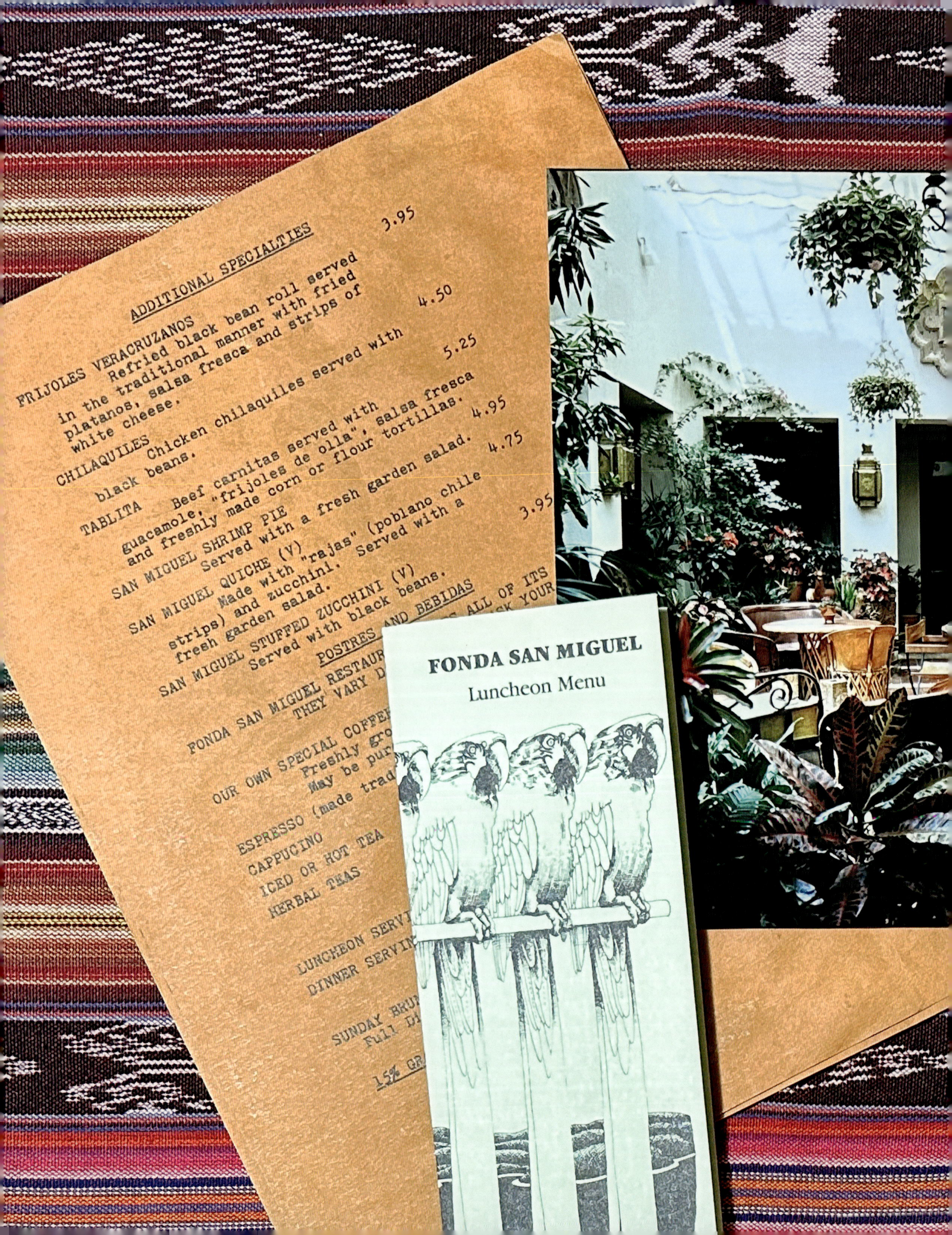

ADDITIONAL SPECIALTIES
FRIJOLES VERACRUZANOS 3.95
Refried black bean roll served in the traditional manner with fried platanos, salsa fresca and strips of white cheese.
CHILAQUILES Chicken chilaquiles served with black beans. 4.50
TABLITA Beef carnitas served with guacamole, "frijoles de olla", salsa fresca and freshly made corn or flour tortillas. 5.25
SAN MIGUEL SHRIMP PIE Served with a fresh garden salad. 4.95
SAN MIGUEL QUICHE (V) Made with "rajas" (poblano chile strips) and zucchini. Served with a fresh garden salad. 4.75
SAN MIGUEL STUFFED ZUCCHINI (V) Served with black beans. 3.95
POSTRES AND BEBIDAS
CAPPUCINO
ICED OR HOT TEA
HERBAL TEAS
FONDA SAN MIGUEL
Luncheon Menu

BAR
MENU
SAN MIGUEL
RESTAURANT
2330 W. NORTH LOOP
Austin, Texas.

During the restaurant's first year, in 1976 (previous page), the atrium was transformed to its present open-air style, featuring a glass ceiling and colorful walls designed by the late Bill Luft and retired University of Texas architecture professor Sinclair Black. Lush greenery and comfortable seating create the feel of a courtyard, traditionally found in many Mexican homes.

Pat Sharpe

Texas Monthly Restaurant Critic, Retired

"Admirers of Fonda San Miguel rightly point to its pioneering work in introducing regional Mexican dishes to a state that had grown up on Tex-Mex. But I wish to pay tribute not just to its remarkable kitchen and cooks but to the gorgeous building they occupy. Before Fonda opened, that structure was a plain white concrete box. Almost immediately, co-founders Tom Gilliland and the late Miguel Ravago began a decades-long transformation that converted it, little by little, into a fantastical Mexican hacienda. Its soaring spaces are filled with hand-painted tiles, tropical plants, and work by leading Mexican artists. Its patio is alluring, with dark, romantic corners. Thanks to their efforts and vision, it is one of the most original and delightful dining venues in the country and a true work of art itself."

Section One

BUILDING BLOCKS

MASA Y PAN

MASA HARINA CORN TORTILLAS

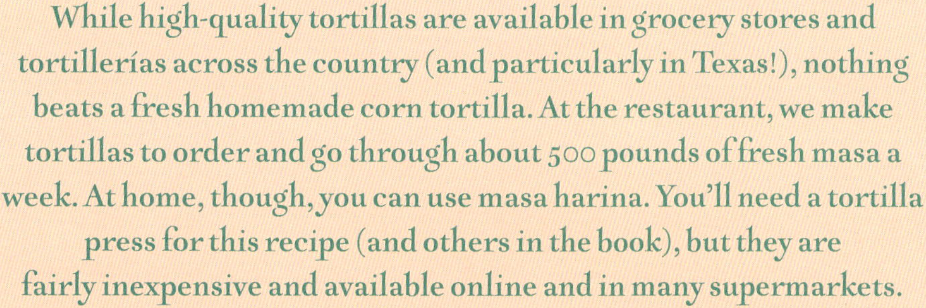

While high-quality tortillas are available in grocery stores and tortillerías across the country (and particularly in Texas!), nothing beats a fresh homemade corn tortilla. At the restaurant, we make tortillas to order and go through about 500 pounds of fresh masa a week. At home, though, you can use masa harina. You'll need a tortilla press for this recipe (and others in the book), but they are fairly inexpensive and available online and in many supermarkets.

Makes 10 to 12 tortillas

1 cup (120g) masa harina
¾ cup (180mL) warm water

1 Add the masa harina to a bowl and slowly add the water. You may not need all of it. Knead the dough until it is well incorporated and there are no more signs of dry powder left. If needed, add up to ¼ cup more water. You want the dough to be moist, but not sticky, about the consistency of playdough.

2 Divide the dough into 10 to 12 equal portions, depending on how large you'd like the tortillas to be. Roll these into round balls.

3 Heat a comal over medium heat while you press your tortillas.

4 To make the tortillas, lay a plastic liner on the open press. Plastic bags from the grocery store are perfect for this. You can also use plastic wrap or resealable plastic bags that have been cut open at the seams.

5 Place a masa ball in the center of the press, and push down on it with your hand to flatten it slightly.

6 Cover the top of the dough with the other piece of plastic, and close the tortilla press all the way.

7 Remove the top piece of plastic and flip the masa onto your hand. Remove the other piece of plastic.

8 In a slow sweeping motion, lay the masa onto the heated comal.

9 Cook for 20 seconds, then flip the tortilla. You'll notice steam coming out from under the sides when it's ready to flip. Cook the other side for 15 to 20 seconds, until again you see a little bit of steam. Keep warm in a tortilla holder while you cook the rest of the tortillas.

Tetelas

TETELAS

These triangular treats are common in Oaxaca, and they're fairly easy to make at home. At the restaurant, we use many colors of masa for visual interest and occasionally even swirl different colors together.

Makes 12

1 pound (450g) fresh masa or masa from masa harina
2 cups (480g) cold Frijoles Refritos (page 98)
1 tomato, diced (about 1 cup or 150g)
½ cup (50g) thinly sliced radishes
½ cup (60g) crumbled queso fresco or cotija cheese
½ cup (25g) shredded lettuce
½ cup (120g) sour cream, at room temperature

1 Divide the masa into 12 equal portions and roll them into balls. You want a very pliable masa; if it's too dry, work in a tablespoon of water at a time until the balls are very smooth when you roll them.

2 Line a tortilla press with two pieces of plastic wrap. One at a time, press the masa very thin, as though you are making tortillas.

3 Carefully peel off the top layer of plastic wrap and use the bottom layer to move the masa to a work surface. Spoon two tablespoons refried beans into the center of the dough. Use the bottom edge of the plastic to fold one side of the masa to the center of the beans. Rotate the tortilla ⅓ of the way around and repeat this fold; rotate ⅓ again and repeat. You should end up with a triangle and not be able to see the beans. Press on the seams lightly to seal. Repeat with remaining masa balls. The sides of the triangle will be between 3 and 4 inches long.

4 Heat a comal or cast-iron pan over medium-high heat.

5 Cook the Tetelas seam-side down for about 2 minutes, then flip and cook for 2 more minutes, until the masa is cooked through. You will likely need to work in batches; remove cooked Tetelas to a kitchen towel and wrap them to keep warm while you finish cooking.

6 Garnish the Tetelas with tomato, radishes, cheese, lettuce, and sour cream, and serve.

1 Divide the masa into 12 equal portions and roll them into balls. Line a tortilla press with two pieces of plastic wrap and place one ball at a time in center.

2 Press the masa very thin, as though you are making tortillas. Carefully peel off the top layer of plastic wrap. Spoon two tablespoons refried beans into the center of the dough.

3 Use the bottom edge of the plastic to fold one side of the masa to the center of the beans.

4 Rotate the tortilla ⅓ of the way around and repeat this fold.

5 Rotate ⅓ again and repeat. You should end up with a triangle and not be able to see the beans. Press on the seams lightly to seal.

SALBUTES

These puffed and fried masa discs are from Yucatán, where they are filled with chicken, beef, pork, vegetables, or a combination. Here, they are served with Pollo Pibil Yucatán and fresh toppings including avocado, Cebollas en Escabeche, queso fresco, and Pico de Gallo.

Makes 12

Canola oil, for frying
1 pound (450g) fresh masa or masa from masa harina (page 31)
Salt, to taste
2 cups (480g) Pollo Pibil Yucatán (page 115), warmed
1 avocado, sliced
½ cup (50g) Cebollas en Escabeche (page 95), drained
½ cup (60g) shredded queso fresco
½ cup (120g) Pico de Gallo (page 57)

1 Heat 2 inches of oil to 350°F in a deep cast-iron skillet, Dutch oven, or other heavy-bottomed pan. Set up a sheet pan lined with paper towels next to the pan.

2 Divide the dough into 12 equal portions and roll into balls. Wetting your hands or rubbing your palms with shortening or lard will help with the stickiness.

3 Line a tortilla press with plastic wrap and press each ball of masa to about ¾ inch thick. They should become 3-inch wide discs.

4 One at a time, fry the masa discs in oil, using a spoon to baste them, until they puff up, about 90 seconds. Use a slotted spoon to remove the Salbutes to the paper towel-lined sheet pan. Sprinkle lightly with salt.

5 Top the Salbutes, in this order, dividing the toppings evenly amongst them: Pollo Pibil Yucatán, avocado, Cebollas en Escabeche, cheese, and Pico de Gallo. Serve warm.

Oscar Alvarez, second from left, and Natalie Gazaui working with Tamales Madre staff.

Tamales Madre

It is said that the most valuable treasures often are hidden in the smallest spaces. That's certainly true for Tamales Madre in Mexico City, whose modest size cannot convey the extent of the culinary experience that awaits those who step inside. In 2024, Fonda San Miguel kitchen staff members traveled to Mexico City for a hands-on class in the step-by-step process of making tamales. It was one of many trips to Mexico's culinary centers, where our chefs soak up authentic cooking techniques and learn how regional spices and fresh locally sourced ingredients can enhance their own cooking skills at Fonda San Miguel.

While corn is the main ingredient of masa, the Tamales Madre team prides itself on offering different varieties of corn to create an assortment of masa flavors. Each provides a unique pairing with different fillings. Even the selection and preparation of hojas, or husks, are important steps in the time-honored tradition of making tamales.

The Tamales Madres team includes Chef Ruben Amador, who is eager to share his deep passion for Mexican gastronomy along with his love of good conversation. Also lending culinary skills is Edher Ortega, one of the newest and most energetic members of the team. The classroom and kitchen spaces may be small, but the enthusiasm and dedication of the team are unlimited at Tamales Madres. It's a welcoming place to learn and sample some of the best tamales ever, making travels to Mexico City worth repeating to share lessons learned with patrons of Fonda San Miguel.

TAMALES

Tamales are versatile. You can change the salsa or filling, and they can be savory or sweet (see the Tamales de Chocolate on page 224). You can change the wrapping to impact flavor, whether you use banana leaves, corn husks, or parchment paper. At Fonda San Miguel, we're inspired by the spongy, fluffy tamal technique Diana Kennedy used.

Makes 12 tamales

½ pound (225g) lard or vegetable shortening, softened
2 tablespoons salt, plus more to taste
1 teaspoon baking powder
1 pound (450g) fresh masa dough (store-bought is fine, but do not buy "masa for tamales")
2 cups (480mL) chicken broth (Caldo de Pollo Básico, page 99, or store-bought), as needed

1 In a mixer fitted with the paddle attachment, whip the lard with the salt and baking powder. Mix on high until the lard turns white, about 1 minute.

2 Turn off the mixer, scrape down the sides with a spatula, and resume mixing on low.

3 Add the masa in pieces, mixing until combined. Slowly pour in chicken broth as needed to create a thick, moist batter while continuing to mix on low.

4 Turn the mixing speed up to medium and mix until all is well incorporated. It should be the consistency of play-dough. Turn off the mixer and scrape down the sides.

5 Give the masa a taste to see if it needs more salt and adjust as needed. You want it to taste slightly oversalted, as the flavor will fade during cooking.

To assemble tamales using banana leaves

1 Prepare your banana leaves by cutting them into 1-foot sections. With a gas stove, heat the leaves over the flame for 5 to 8 seconds. The texture will change, becoming more pliable. With a microwave oven, wrap 10 to 12 cut banana leaves first in a wet paper towel, then in plastic wrap. Microwave in 30-second increments, checking between each to see if the leaves have become pliable.

2 Add about ½ cup of masa to the center of a banana leaf. Spread the masa out slightly with the back of a spoon, leaving ½ inch of banana leaf exposed on all edges. Add about 2 tablespoons filling to the middle of the masa.

3 Fold the banana leaf in thirds lengthwise, by folding the close end up, then folding the far end toward you. Then carefully fold the sides underneath to seal the masa in. Wrap with twine or strands of banana leaf if you think it needs to be more secure.

4 Set up a tamale steamer by bringing 1 or 2 inches of water in the bottom of a large pot to a simmer and setting a steamer tray or rack in the pot. Do not allow the water to touch the bottom of the rack. Place the tamales in the steam pan turned on low, as you go.

5 Once all the tamales are wrapped, turn steamer on high and close the lid tightly. Steam for 40 to 50 minutes.

6 Serve warm.

To assemble tamales using corn husks

1 Prepare your corn husks by soaking them in water overnight. If you don't have time for that, place them in a large bowl and pour hot water over them, soaking them for about 1 hour. In both cases, make sure the husks are fully immersed. You may need to place a weight on them to prevent them from floating.

2 Once all the husks are pliable, you are ready to start assembling. Use the larger husks, with the silky side facing up.

3 With a spoon add about ¼ cup of masa to the center of the husk. Spread the masa out slightly, being careful not to spread too close to the ends. Add 1 to 2 tablespoons filling to the middle of the masa. This is easiest to do holding in your dominant hand. (For small corn husks, put in less masa and filling.)

4 Fold over one side of the husk to the end of the masa, then fold over the other side to wrap around as much as possible. Think of wrapping yourself in a robe. Then fold the top of the tamal to seal.

5 Place the tamales in your steam pan with water, turned on low, as you go.

6 Once all the tamales are wrapped, turn steamer on high and close the lid tightly. Steam for 40 to 50 minutes.

8 Serve warm.

Sfihas with Toum

SFIHAS

Sfihas came to Mexico with Lebanese immigrants, who began moving to the country in the 19th century. Sfihas can be filled with all kinds of stuffings, but this recipe calls for a traditional spiced meat mixture made with half beef and half lamb.

Makes 12 Sfihas

Sfiha Dough

1 ¾ cups (220g) all-purpose flour, plus additional flour for dusting your work surface
5 teaspoons milk powder
5 teaspoons granulated sugar
1 teaspoon kosher salt
1 teaspoon instant yeast
2 tablespoons extra virgin olive oil, plus more to brush on Sfihas
1 large egg, at room temperature
½ cup (120mL) water

1 Combine flour, milk powder, sugar, salt, and yeast in a large bowl.
2 Add the oil and egg, and stir to combine
3 Slowly add water until the dough comes together. You may not need to add all the water.
4 Knead the dough in the bowl 8 to 10 times.
5 Cover the bowl with plastic or a clean towel. Let rise for 30 minutes.
6 Heat oven to 350°F.
7 Divide the dough into 12 equal pieces and roll into balls.
8 Use a rolling pin to flatten each ball into a circle the thickness of a pie crust, about 4 inches across.

Sfiha Filling

1 tablespoon butter*
½ cup (75g) finely diced white onion
2 cloves garlic, chopped
1 large Roma tomato, seeds removed, finely diced
½ pound (225g) ground beef or lamb (or combination of both)
1 teaspon kosher salt, or to taste
½ teaspon cinnamon
½ teaspon allspice
¼ teaspon chile de árbol powder
1 tablespoon sumac
1 tablespoon lemon juice
1 tablespoon roughly chopped mint
1 tablespoon roughly chopped parsley
1 tablespoon roughly chopped cilantro
3 tablespoons tahini
1 tablespoon pomegranate molasses
1 tablespoon labneh (or equal parts whole plain yogurt and sour cream)

1 In butter, sauté onion, garlic, and tomatoes until softened, about 5 minutes.
2 Add the meat and brown, stirring constantly to break up the meat, about 8 minutes.
3 Add remaining ingredients. Stir well, taste, and adjust salt if needed.
4 Remove from heat and let cool completely. Refrigerate for at least 30 minutes before filling the Sfihas.

**Note: Traditionally clarified butter is used here.*

Making the Sfihas

½ cup (120mL) labneh
½ cup (120mL) Toum

1 Add a generous spoonful of Sfiha filling in the middle of each piece of dough.
2 Fold up four sides of the dough to hug the filling and pinch the corners to stick them together, creating squares of dough with pinched corners and the filling exposed on top.
3 Place the Sfihas on a parchment-lined sheet tray.
4 Brush olive oil on each. Repinch corners if they lose their shape.
5 Bake 15 to 20 minutes, until the dough begins to turn golden.
6 While the Sfihas are baking, whisk together the labneh and Toum for the sauce.
7 Let cool slightly and serve with the sauce on the side.

Toum

Makes about 2 cups
1 cup (130g) garlic cloves, green part removed
1 tablespoon sour orange juice
1 ¾ cups (420mL) canola oil
Salt, to taste
Lemon juice, to taste

1 Puree the garlic and sour orange juice in a food processor or blender. Slowly drizzle in the oil until a mayonnaise-like sauce forms.
2 Season with salt and lemon juice to taste.

22
EL GLUTEN
31
EL TROLL

9
EL BARRIL
1

Hombre con pipa. Rufino Tamayo.

PEDRO FRIEDEBERG '72

Four works by Pedro Friedeberg.

Fiesta + Cena. Leovigildo Martinez.

Mujer y Angeles. Manokergica

Untitled. Javier Maximiliano.

Dimensional painting. Sergio Bustamante.

Tiles in the men's rest room at Fonda San Miguel are from Austin Clay Imports and feature the millennial generation's take on the traditional game of lotería, or bingo, which was introduced to Mexico in the 1770s.

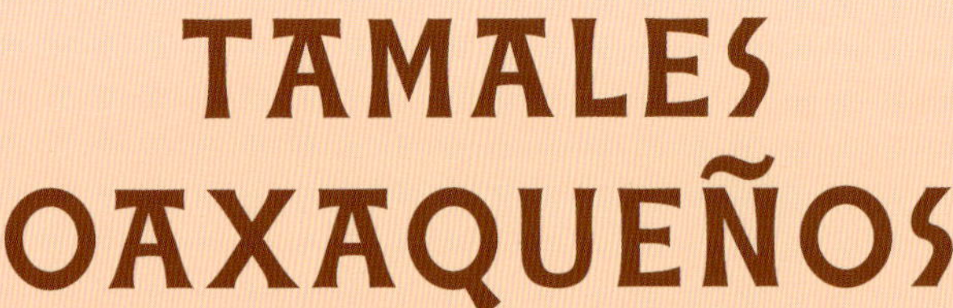

TAMALES OAXAQUEÑOS

These simple tamales comprise just beans and masa, but they are layered into a spiral that becomes visible when you cut into the tamale. It's a visually striking treat that was traditionally eaten at the end of the harvest but is tasty year-round.

Makes 12 tamales

2 cups (480mL) water
2 chiles de árbol, seeds removed for a milder dish
2 cups (560g) Frijoles Refritos (page 98)
1 pound (450g) fresh masa
12 corn husks, soaked in hot water for about 10 minutes
1 leaf hoja santa, torn into 1 ½-inch pieces

1 In a small pot, boil 2 cups of water. Remove from heat, add the chiles, and soak for 20 minutes.

2 Prepare steam pot for the tamales (see page 42).

3 Place the chiles in a blender with just enough chile soaking water to puree them.

4 Add the Frijoles Refritos to the chile puree and blend on high. Add 1 tablespoon of fresh water at a time to help the mixture blend better, as needed.

5 Line a tortilla press with 2 sheets of plastic, and place a 2-ounce ball of masa (about the size of a golf ball) in the middle. Press the dough all the way down, as if making tortillas. Pivot the masa 45 degrees and press down again. Remove the top piece of plastic.

6 See pages 52 and 53 for instructions on how to make these tamales.

7 Fold the corn husk so as to completely cover the tamal. Take the very tip of the husk, and fold it over toward the bottom. Stack the tamales vertically in the steamer, open end pointing up, as you go. When the pan is full, steam the tamales for 40 minutes.

1 Use the plastic tortilla press liner to move the masa circle to a work surface.

2 Use a spoon to spread 2 tablespoons of beans to about ½ inch from the edge of the masa.

3 Use the plastic on the side closest to you to fold the masa over about ⅓ of the way.

4 Once folded, peel plastic off masa before proceeding to next step.

5 Use the plastic on the side farthest from you to fold up the masa.

6 Press the masa layers lightly to seal. Peel plastic off masa before proceeding to next step.

7 Cut the tamale in half crosswise.

8 Spread another tablespoon of the puree directly onto the tamal. Press a small piece of hoja santa into the puree.

9 Wrap the husk around the tamal.

10 Tuck the bottom of the husk under the tamal.

11 Steam the tamales stacked vertically for 40 minutes and serve.

SALSAS Y SAUCES

Salsa Roja de Mesa

Salsa de Poblano y Aguacate

Pico de Gallo

Salsa de Jitomate

Salsa Verde
de Mesa
Salsa Macha
Salsa Morita
Salsa Habanero
Salsa Rustica

SALSA RUSTICA

Try this basic red table salsa from Michoacán that is great to have on hand for many different types of dishes.

Makes about 3½ cups

5 large Roma tomatoes
½ white onion
3 cloves garlic
½ serrano, stem removed
Salt, to taste

1 Heat a skillet or cast-iron pan over medium heat. Char the tomatoes and onion in a dry pan until lightly charred all over, 15 to 20 minutes, turning them periodically.
2 Add them with garlic and serrano to a blender or food processor. Pulse until combined and evenly chopped—you want it to be chunky.
3 Season with salt to taste.

SALSA ROJA DE MESA

The house salsa at Fonda San Miguel, originally created by Chef Miguel Ravago, can be customized at home to your preferred spice level. Removing seeds from the chiles reduces the spice level. At the restaurant, we typically remove the seeds from half the chiles we use.

Makes about 3 cups

4 large Roma tomatoes, roughly chopped
½ medium white onion, roughly chopped
2 to 4 serranos, depending on desired spice level
1 clove garlic, chopped
Salt, to taste
1 tablespoon canola oil

1 Heat oven to 350°F.
2 In a roasting pan, add the tomatoes, onion, serranos, and garlic, and cook for 10 to 12 minutes, until softened.
3 In a molcajete or food processor, combine the roasted vegetables and salt. If using the food processor, pulse the vegetables for a chunkier salsa.
4 In a saucepan, heat the oil on a medium heat.
5 Add the salsa to the pan, reduce the heat to low and simmer for 5 minutes.
6 Serve warm or refrigerate for later use.

SALSA VERDE DE MESA

Add diced avocado to Chef Miguel Ravago's original recipe when you serve this as a table salsa. But as a sauce for enchiladas or other dishes, it is better without.

Makes about 3½ cups

6 medium tomatillos, husks removed
4 serranos, stems removed (2 cooked, 2 raw)
Water to cover
5 sprigs cilantro
1 clove garlic
¼ medium white onion
Salt, to taste
1 tablespoon canola oil
Sugar, to taste
1 small avocado, diced, if desired

1 In a saucepan, add the tomatillos and 2 serranos, cover with water, and bring to a boil. Lower the heat and simmer until the green of the tomatillos begins to fade, about 8 minutes.
2 Drain the water from the tomatillos, reserving 1 cup of the cooking liquid.
3 In a blender, combine the tomatillos, cooking liquid, serranos (both cooked and raw), cilantro, garlic, onion, and salt, and puree until nearly smooth.
4 Heat the oil in a saucepan on medium. Add the salsa, and simmer for 8 minutes. If the salsa is bit bitter, add sugar to remove the flavor.
5 Add avocado, adjust the seasoning if necessary, and serve warm or chilled.

PICO DE GALLO

Pico de Gallo is a classic for a reason! Fonda San Miguel garnishes all kinds of dishes with Pico, but it's great on its own with warm tostada chips.

Makes about 1 quart

4 large Roma tomatoes, finely diced
½ white onion, finely diced
1 serrano, seeds removed, minced
½ bunch cilantro, roughly chopped
Juice of 2 limes
Salt, to taste

1 Add the tomatoes, onion, serrano, and cilantro to a bowl and mix well to combine.
2 Add the lime juice little by little until it tastes good to you—you may need only one lime.
3 Add salt to taste, and refrigerate for at least 30 minutes before serving.

SALSA HABANERO

This one can be quite spicy. In this version, the nuts add a creamy note for balance.

Makes 1 quart

1 to 2 habaneros, stems removed, seeds removed if you prefer a milder salsa
5 Roma tomatoes
2 tablespoons roasted unsalted almonds
2 tablespoons pepitas
1 clove garlic
¼ white onion, roughly chopped
Salt, to taste

1 Blend all ingredients in a blender until smooth.
2 Salt to taste.

SALSA MACHA

Salsa Macha, an oil-based salsa full of dried chiles and nuts, is enjoying a surge in popularity. This version, from Fonda San Miguel Senior Cook Oscar Alvarez, is unique in that it contains more nuts than most. Feel free to experiment with whatever nuts you have on hand. This version contains peanuts, almonds, sesame seeds, and pepitas, any of which can be left out if allergies are an issue.

Makes 1 quart

3 cups (720mL) canola oil
¼ cup (25g) roughly chopped morita chiles
¼ cup (25g) roughly chopped chiles de árbol
½ cup (70g) peanuts
½ cup almonds (70g), any kind will do (slivered, whole, sliced)
¼ cup (35g) sesame seeds
½ cup (70g) pepitas
¼ cup (30g) garlic cloves, roughly chopped
2 tablespoons brown sugar
1 tablespoon salt

1 Set a large heavy skillet over medium heat and add the oil. Don't allow it to smoke.
2 Once the oil is hot and shimmering, add the morita chiles. Stir for about 1 minute, until the chiles start to gain color.
3 Add the chiles de árbol and stir for 30 seconds.
4 Add the peanuts and almonds, stir for about 2 minutes.
5 Add the sesame seeds, pepitas, and garlic, and stir for about 1 minute.
6 Remove from heat, and add the brown sugar and salt. Allow to cool.
7 Store Salsa Macha in a jar, refrigerated.

CREMA DE AGUACATE

This is a simple puree that dresses up dishes like the Tiradito Mayan on page 153.

Makes about ¾ cup

1 ripe avocado
Juice of 1 lime
1 tablespoon salt, plus more to taste
½ cup (120mL) water

1 In a blender add the first three ingredients.
2 Blend and add water slowly to help thin and make a smooth puree.

SALSA DE POBLANO Y AGUACATE

More complex and spicy than the Crema de Aguacate, this sauce works well on tacos, enchiladas, and more. Note that some recipes in this book call for the heavy cream to be left out of this sauce.

Makes about 3 cups

1 large or 2 small avocados
2 tomatillos, husks removed, quartered
½ poblano pepper, roasted, peeled, and seeds and stem removed
Juice of 1 lime
½ bunch cilantro
2 tablespoons roughly chopped white onion
1 clove garlic
1 serrano pepper, seeds removed for a milder salsa
½ cup (120mL) water
1 cup (240mL) heavy cream
Salt, to taste

1 Blend all of the ingredients on high speed until smooth.
2 Season to taste.

A tile mural featuring an altar to Our Lady of Guadalupe, the Patron Saint of Mexico, and San Pascual Bailón, the patron saint of cooks (large figure in center), was part of the extensive remodel of a key restaurant attraction, the tortilla station. Customers enjoy watching tortillas de masa y harina being made daily. The late Rodolfo González and his son, Gorky, made the all beautiful tiles that line the walls.

SALSA MORITA

Morita chiles, which are smoked and dried jalapeños, are worth seeking out for this flavorful salsa.

Makes 1 quart

3 pounds (1.36kg) Roma tomatoes, about 10
1½ pounds (680g) tomatillos, about 10, husks removed and cleaned
6 cloves garlic
5 to 6 morita chiles, depending on size/spice level desired
Salt, to taste

1 Heat oven to 425°F.
2 Roast tomatoes and tomatillos on a sheet pan until charred in places, about 45 minutes. Remove from oven and let cool.
3 Blend the tomatoes, tomatillos, garlic, and moritas in a blender until smooth. Season to taste.

SALSA DE JITOMATE

This is an all-purpose red salsa with a customizable spice level—add as many (or few) serranos as you like!

Makes 1 quart

5 pounds (2.25kg) Roma tomatoes, about 15
2 tablespoons vegetable oil
1 white onion, diced
6 cloves garlic, minced
2 to 3 serranos, stems removed, finely diced
Salt, to taste (approximately 1 tablespoon)

1 In a dry skillet or cast-iron pan, roast the tomatoes over medium-high heat until softened and charred in places, about 15 minutes. Remove from heat.
2 Heat the vegetable oil in a skillet (this can be the pan you used to roast the tomatoes), and sauté the onion, garlic, and serranos over medium heat until translucent, about 10 minutes.
3 Blend the hot tomatoes and sautéed vegetables at high speed until emulsified and smooth, about 3 minutes. Season with salt to taste.

VEGAN MAYO CHIPOTLE

Try this vegan salsa with Tacos de Coliflor, on page 131, for a vegan entree. Or you can use regular mayonnaise, if that's what you have on hand.

Makes about 1 cup

2 chipotle chiles en adobo
Juice of 1 lime
¼ white onion, roughly chopped
4 cloves garlic
1 cup (240g) vegan mayonnaise (may substitute vegan sour cream)
Salt, to taste (optional)

1 In a blender, add the chiles, lime juice, onion, and garlic. Blend to make a paste.
2 Add the mayonnaise and blend until uniform. If you need additional seasoning, salt to taste.

QUESO VEGANO

The key to this vegan queso, it turns out, is butternut squash, which gives it that vibrant queso color without the cheese. This stands well on its own with tostadas, or combine it in equal parts with the Salsa Verde de Mesa, on page 57, for a vegan enchilada sauce (see Enchiladas Suizas de Hongos, page 196).

Makes 1 quart

2 cups (300g) cubed butternut squash
2 cups (200 to 250g) roughly chopped cauliflower
½ cup (75g) corn kernels
4 cups (960mL) unsweetened almond milk (or enough to cover vegetables)
¾ teaspoon ground cumin
1 ½ teaspoon garlic powder
1 ½ teaspoon onion powder
6 ounces (170g) vegan cheddar cheese, shredded
Salt, to taste

1 Add the squash, cauliflower, corn, almond milk, cumin, garlic powder, and onion powder to a large saucepan. Bring the mixture to a boil, then reduce the heat to medium-low and simmer for 20 minutes. Check to see if the butternut squash is tender and finished cooking. Remove the pot from heat.
2 Use a slotted spoon to carefully add the cooked vegetables to the blender, then add the cooking liquid until it comes halfway up the vegetables. (Reserve leftover cooking liquid.) Puree the vegetables until smooth.
3 Add the vegan cheese and blend on high, until the sauce becomes a smooth puree. Add cooking liquid for a consistency slightly thinner than pancake batter.
4 Season and serve. Store refrigerated for up to 5 days.

Mole Blanco ingredients

MOLES

MOLE BLANCO

This mole was inspired by Olga Cabrera. Numerous ingredients come together to build a rich, layered sauce. Like most moles, this is often served for celebrations, typically Christmas and Easter.

Makes about 4 quarts

1 small white/yellow carrot, peeled and diced
5 cloves garlic, chopped
¼ white onion, diced
½ cup (115g) manteca lard, divided
½ calabacita, peeled and diced
¼ fennel bulb, diced, fronds removed and reserved
2 white plums, peeled and diced
1 small apple, peeled and diced
1 cup (120g) ½-inch cauliflower florets
1 small serrano
1 small habanero
1 white banana pepper
1 plantain, peeled and diced
½ cup (60g) almonds
½ cup (75g) sesame seeds
½ cup (75g) pine nuts
½ cup (70g) cashews
½ cup (80g) golden raisins
2 white corn tortillas, torn into pieces
Infused Herb Oil
2 cups (480mL) chicken stock
¼ cup (45g) white chocolate chips
Salt, to taste

1 In a large pot over medium heat, sauté the carrot, garlic, and onion in ¼ cup lard until soft, about 3 minutes.
2 Add the calabacita, fennel, plums, apple, cauliflower, serrano, habanero, banana pepper, and plantain, turn the heat to low, and sauté for 7 minutes, until cooked about halfway through.
3 Add the almonds, sesame seeds, pine nuts, cashews, and raisins, and cook for 7 minutes. Stir constantly to prevent the mixture from burning.
4 Add the tortillas, Infused Herb Oil, and stock, and simmer for 30 minutes.
5 Puree mixture in a blender until smooth.
6 Heat the remaining ¼ cup lard in the pot over medium-low heat and carefully pour in the puree through a mesh strainer. Cook, stirring frequently, for about 15 minutes. Whisk in the chocolate chips until melted, salt to taste, and serve.

Infused Herb Oil

Yields ⅔ cup

½ bunch cilantro
¼ bunch epazote
10 sprigs thyme, leaves picked and stems discarded
Reserved fennel fronds from the mole ingredients (about ¼ cup, 5g)
4 cloves garlic
1 cup (240mL) canola oil
½ teaspoon salt

1 Blend together all ingredients for 2 minutes on high speed.
2 Strain the oil through a fine mesh sieve lined with cheese cloth for a perfectly smooth oil. Store in the refrigerator for up to 2 days, or freeze.

MOLE BLANCO

Este mole también se inspiró en Olga Cabrera. Decenas de ingredientes se unen para crear una salsa rica y compleja. Como la mayoría de los moles, este se suele servir en celebraciones, normalmente en Navidad o Pascua.

Rinde unos 4 cuartos (3.5-4 litros)

1 zanahoria amarilla o blanca pequeña, pelada y cortada en dados
5 dientes de ajo, picados
¼ de una cebolla blanca, cortada en dados
½ taza (115 g) de manteca, dividida
½ calabacita, pelada y cortada en dados
¼ de un bulbo de hinojo, cortado en dados, las frondas retiradas y reservadas
2 ciruelas amarillas o verdes, peladas y cortadas en dados
1 manzana pequeña, pelada y cortada en dados
1 taza (120g) de ramilletes de coliflor de 1 cm
1 chile serrano pequeño
1 chile habanero pequeño
1 chile güero
1 plátano macho, pelado y cortado en dados
½ taza (60g) de almendras
½ taza (75g) de ajonjolí
½ taza (75g) de piñones
½ taza (70g) de nuez de la India
½ taza (80g) de pasas sultanas
2 tortillas de maíz blanca, hechas trozos
Aceite infusionado con hierbas, receta a continuación
2 tazas (480ml) de caldo de pollo
¼ taza(45g) de chispas de chocolate blanco
Sal, al gusto

1 En una olla grande a fuego medio, saltea la zanahoria, el ajo y la cebolla en una ¼ taza de la manteca hasta que se ablanden, unos 3 minutos.
2 Agrega la calabacita, el hinojo, las ciruelas, la manzana, el coliflor, el chile serrano, el chile habanero, el chile güero y el plátano macho, pon el fuego a bajo y sofríe durante 7 minutos, hasta que las verduras estén medio cocidas.
3 Añade las almendras, el ajonjolí, los piñones, la nuez de la India y las pasas sultanas y cuece otros 7 minutos. Remueve constantemente para evitar que la mezcla se queme.
4 Agrega la tortilla, el aceite de hierbas y el caldo, lleva la mezcla hasta el punto de hervir y cuece a fuego lento durante 30 minutos.
5 Tritura esta mezcla en una licuadora hasta que quede suave.
6 Calienta el ¼ de manteca restante en la olla a fuego medio bajo y vierte con cuidado el puré por un colador de malla. Cuece, removiendo con frecuencia, durante unos 15 minutos. Incorpora las chispas de chocolate hasta que se derritan, pon sal al gusto y sirve.

Aceite Infusionado con Hierbas

Rinde ⅔ taza

Medio manojo de cilantro
Cuarto manojo de epazote
10 ramitas de tomillo, las hojas recogidas y los tallos desechados
Las frondas del hinojo reservadas de los ingredientes del molo (aproximadamente ¼ de taza, 5g)
4 dientes de ajo
1 taza (240ml) de aceite de canola
½ cucharadita de sal

1 Mezclar todos los ingredientes durante 2 minutos a alta velocidad.
2 Cuela el aceite por un colador de malla fina forrada con manta de cielo para obtener un aceite perfectamente liso. Guárdalo en la refrigerador hasta dos días o congélalo.

CHICHILO DE CHICHAROS

Chichilo is named for the chile that flavors this mole: chilhuacle negro. This is another black mole, which gets its color from charring several ingredients and is typically served with beef, pork, or a mixture.

Makes 3 ½ cups

¼ teaspoon whole cloves
¼ teaspoon whole black peppercorns
1 teaspoon whole cumin
1 teaspoon oregano
1 teaspoon marjoram
1 teaspoon dried thyme
1 white onion, halved
6 cloves garlic, unpeeled
2 Roma tomatoes
2 tomatillos, husks removed
2 pasillas
4 chiles chilhuacle negro
6 corn tortillas
3 avocado leaves
3 cups (720mL) chicken stock, or enough to cover
1 tablespoon lard or canola oil
Salt, to taste

1 Toast the cloves, black peppercorns, and cumin in a small cast-iron pan, taking care not to burn them, until fragrant. Grind finely in a spice grinder along with the oregano, marjoram, and thyme.
2 Heat a comal or cast-iron pan over medium-high heat. Char the onion, garlic, tomatoes, and tomatillos, flipping occasionally, until blackened in places, and add them to a blender. Do the same with pasillas, chilhuacles, tortillas, and avocado leaves (those will not take as much time). Add them to the blender as well.
3 Cover the charred ingredients with broth and blend until smooth.
4 Heat a sauce pot with lard or oil and "fry" the mole over medium heat for about 20 minutes, stirring frequently, until mole is thick and concentrated. Season with salt to taste.

Rinde 3 ½ tazas (aproximadamente 900 ml)

¼ cucharadita (de clavos de olor enteros
¼ cucharadita de granos de pimienta negra enteras
1 cucharadita de comino entero
1 cucharadita de orégano
1 cucharadita de mejorana
1 cucharadita de tomillo seco
1 cebolla blanca (150g), partida por la mitad
6 dientes de ajo con la cáscara
2 jitomates Roma (saladet)
2 tomatillos (tomates verdes) sin cáscara
2 chiles pasilla
4 chilhuacles negros
6 tortillas de maíz
3 hojas de aguacate
3 tazas de caldo de pollo (720ml), aproximadamente, o suficiente para cubrir
1 cucharada sopera de manteca o aceite de canola (15ml)
Sal, al gusto

1 Tuesta los clavos de olor, los granos de pimienta y el comino en una sartén pequeña de hierro fundido, con cuidado de no quemarlos, hasta que desprendan aroma. Muélelos finamente en un molinillo de especias junto con el orégano, la mejorana y el tomillo seco.
2 Calienta un comal o una sartén de hierro fundido a fuego medio-alto. Asa la cebolla, los dientes de ajo, los jitomates y los tomatillos dándoles la vuelta de vez en cuando hasta que se ennegrezcan en partes, y ponlos en una licuadora. Haz lo mismo con los chiles pasilla, los chilhuacles y las hojas de aguacate (no te llevará tanto tiempo). Agrégalos a la licuadora.
3 Cubre los ingredientes asados con el caldo y licua hasta que queda suave.
4 Calienta la manteca o el aceite en una olla y fríe el mole a fuego medio durante unos 20 minuto, removiéndolo frecuentemente, hasta que el mole sea espeso y concentrado. Sazona con sal al gusto.

SEGUEZA

This is a chunkier mole, cooked for a long time with cracked corn. It is often served with rabbit.

Makes 3 quarts

5 guajillo chiles, stems and seeds removed
1 chile de árbol, stems and seeds removed
Boiling water to cover
1 cup (170g) maize amarillo
6 black peppercorns, freshly ground
4 cloves, freshly ground
1 teaspoon cumin seed, freshly ground
8 cloves garlic, minced
1 hoja santa leaf
¼ cup (40g) roughly chopped white onion
1 ½ teaspoons dried oregano
½ teaspoon dried thyme
¾ cup (180g) quartered Roma tomatoes
1 gallon (3.8L) chicken stock, divided
¼ cup (60mL) vegetable oil
Salt, to taste

1 In a skillet, toast the guajillos and chile de árbol over medium heat until darkened and fragrant, about 4 minutes. Put them in a heat-tolerant bowl and cover with boiling water. Let steep 20 minutes.

2 In a dry skillet, toast the maize over medium heat until it smells like popcorn, about 4 minutes. Add to a blender and pulse to break the corn into small pieces. Remove from the blender.

3 Use a slotted spoon or tongs to move the chiles to the blender; discard the chile water. Add the peppercorns, cloves, cumin, garlic, hoja santa, onion, oregano, thyme, and tomatoes, cover with chicken stock, and puree until smooth.

4 Heat the vegetable oil in a large heavy-bottomed pot. Add the puree and the rest of the chicken stock. Bring to a boil, reduce to a simmer, and whisk in the corn pieces. Simmer for 2 hours, or until the corn is cooked through, season with salt, and serve.

Rinde 3 cuartos (aproximadamente 3 litros)

5 chiles guajillos sin rabos, ni venas ni semillas
1 chile de árbol, sin rabo, ni venas, ni semillas
Agua hirviendo hasta cubrir
1 taza de maíz amarillo (170g)
6 granos de pimienta, recién molidas
4 clavos de olor, recién molidos
1 cucharadita de comino (2g), recién molido
8 dientes de ajo, picados
1 hoja santa
¼ taza de cebolla blanca (40g), picado en trozos grandes
1 ½ cucharaditas de orégano seco
½ cucharadita de tomillo seco
¾ taza jitomate saladet (Roma) (180g), cortados en cuartos
1 galón de caldo de pollo (3.8L)
¼ taza de aceite vegetal (60ml)
Sal, al gusto

1 Tuesta los chiles guajillos y el chile de árbol en una sartén a fuego medio hasta que se oscurezcan y desprendan aroma, unos 4 minutos. Ponlos en un bol refractario y cúbrelos con el agua hirviendo. Deja reposar 20 minutos.

2 En una sartén sin aceite (o en un comal), tuesta el maíz a fuego medio hasta que huela a palomitas, unos 4 minutos. Añade a una licuadora y pulsa para romper el maíz en pedacitos. Retíralo de la licuadora.

3 Utiliza una cuchara ranurada o unas pinzas para mover los chiles a la licuadora y desecha el agua enchilado. Agrega los granos de pimienta, los clavos de olor . el comino, el ajo, la hoja santa, la cebolla, el orégano, el tomillo y los jitomates, cubre con caldo de pollo y licua hasta que queda suave.

4 Caliente el aceite vegetal en una olla grande de fondo grueso. Añade el puré y el resto del caldo de pollo. Llévalo a ebullición, redúcelo a fuego lento e incorpora los trozos de maíz. Cocina a fuego lento durante 2 horas, o hasta que el maíz esté bien cocido, sazona con sal y sirve.

MOLE AMARILLO

This is sometimes called Mole del Día, because it doesn't take very long to make and is best served the day it's made along with pork, chicken, or vegetables.

Makes 2 quarts

6 cups (1.4L) water, divided
12 guajillo chiles, stems and seeds removed
5 tomatillos, husks removed, quartered
9 cloves garlic
½ white onion, roughly chopped
1 tablespoon chopped hoja santa
1 tablespoon dried oregano
1 teaspoon whole allspice, toasted
1 teaspoon whole cloves, toasted
¼ teaspoon whole cumin seeds, toasted
3 tablespoons lard
½ cup (60g) masa
Salt, to taste

1 Boil 4 cups water and pour it over the guajillos in a mixing bowl, to soften.
2 Sauté the tomatillos, garlic, and onion until softened, about 5 minutes.
3 Blend the vegetables with the hoja santa and oregano until smooth.
4 Blend in the allspice, cloves, and cumin seeds on high, then add the guajillos along with 1 cup of the soaking water.
5 Melt the lard in a large pan over medium heat, then "fry" the mole for about 30 minutes, stirring frequently, to develop the flavors and thicken.
6 Add 2 cups of water to the blender and add the masa. Blend on high to puree.
7 Pass the masa water thru a strainer into the mole while whisking. Simmer a few more minutes, season to taste, and serve.

COLORADITO

This less-common mole pairs best with vegetables, particularly roasted carrots.

Makes 1 ½ quarts

4 cups (946mL) water, boiling
12 chiles guajillo, stems and seeds removed
4 tablespoons lard, divided
3 medium Roma tomatoes, cut in quarters
1 small white onion, cut in quarters
10 cloves garlic, smashed
1 plantain, peeled and cut into 1-inch pieces
¼ bolillo bread, torn into pieces
¼ cup (37g) sesame seeds
1 ½ teaspoons oregano
2 whole cloves
2 whole allspice berries
1 cinnamon stick
1 ounce (30g) of Mexican chocolate, such as Abuelita, broken into pieces
Salt, to taste

1 Pour boiling water over the guajillos in a mixing bowl, to soften. Let steep 20 minutes.
2 In a pot, heat 2 tablespoons lard and sauté the tomatoes, onion, garlic, and plantain for 15 to 20 minutes, until everything is broken down to mush. Add the bread and stir until moistened. Remove from heat.
3 In a dry skillet or cast-iron pan, toast the sesame seeds, oregano, cloves, allspice, and cinnamon until fragrant, about 3 minutes. Blend toasted spices into a powder.
4 Drain the guajillos and discard the water. Add the tomato mixture and the softened guajillos to the blender with the spices, and puree together.
5 In a large heavy-bottomed pot, heat remaining lard. Pour the blender mixture into the pot to "fry." Cook it for about 1 hour, stirring frequently, to develop the flavors and thicken. Remove from heat.
6 Add the chocolate to the pot and stir to melt. Salt to taste.

Wait staff member Damry Benitez delivers warm chips and fresh salsa to customers upon their arrival.

MOLE ESTOFADO

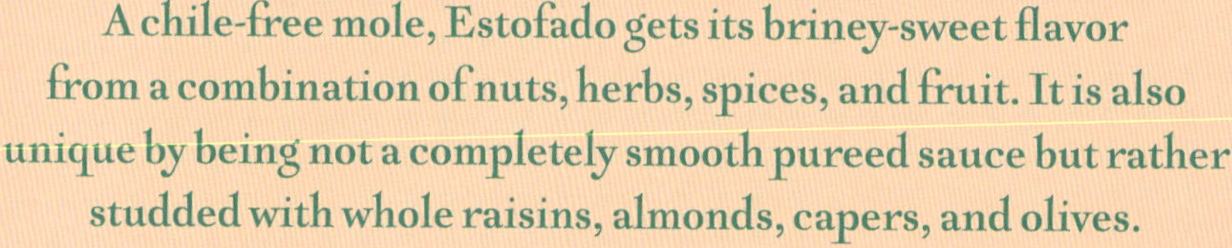

A chile-free mole, Estofado gets its briney-sweet flavor from a combination of nuts, herbs, spices, and fruit. It is also unique by being not a completely smooth pureed sauce but rather studded with whole raisins, almonds, capers, and olives.

Makes about 6 quarts

¼ cup (57g) lard, divided
½ pound tomatillos (2 to 3 tomatillos, depending on size), quartered
½ pound Roma tomatoes (1 to 2 tomatoes, depending on size), quartered
Salt, to taste
1 small white onion, diced
4 cloves garlic, smashed
½ pound (225g) almonds, toasted
½ pound (225g) sesame seeds, toasted
¼ pound plus ¼ cup (170g) raisins, divided
1 ½ teaspoons dried thyme leaves
1 ½ teaspoons black peppercorns
1 ½ teaspoons cloves
1 cinnamon stick
½ teaspoon cumin seeds
3 bay leaves
1 tablespoon dried oregano
1 plantain, peeled and cut into 1-inch pieces
1 corn tortilla, torn into pieces
12 to 15 cups (2.8L to 3.5L) water
¼ cup (35g) capers
¼ cup (40g) chopped green olives
¼ cup (25g) sliced almonds
2 tablespoons brown sugar
¼ to ½ cup (60 to 120mL) Escabeche Brine (page 93) or distilled white vinegar, to taste

1 In a large skillet or cast-iron pan, heat 2 tablespoons lard on medium-low heat and cook the tomatillos and tomatoes on low for about 30 minutes, stirring occasionally until tomatoes completely break down. Salt to taste. Puree in a blender and return to the pan. Keep the tomatoes on a low simmer to reduce while you make the rest of the mole.

2 Heat 2 tablespoons of lard in a large deep pot over medium heat, and sauté the onions and garlic until the onions are translucent, about 5 minutes.

3 Add the toasted almonds, sesame seeds, ½ pound raisins, thyme, peppercorns, cloves, cinnamon stick, cumin, bay leaves, and oregano to the onion pan. Cook for 2 minutes, then add the plantain and tortilla. Cook for about 30 minutes. The mix will get darker.

4 Working in batches, blend the nut and seed mixture with enough water to emulsify it into a smooth paste. (At this point, the base can be cooled and frozen for later use if needed.)

5 Strain the nut puree through a mesh strainer back into the pot, and cook for 30 to 45 minutes. It will continue to get darker.

6 Pass the tomato mixture through the strainer and into the nut mixture. Stir well. Simmer on low to thicken, about 20 minutes. Pass this through a fine mesh strainer.

7 Add the capers, olives, ¼ cup raisins, and sliced almonds to the mole.

8 Add brown sugar and additional salt if needed. Add Escabeche Brine, to taste.

MOLE ESTOFADO

El estofado, un mole sin chile, obtiene su sabor dulce y salado de una combinación de frutos secos, hierbas y especias, plátanos, pasas, alcaparras y aceitunas. También es único porque no es una salsa completamente suave y hecha puré, sino que está salpicada de pasas enteras, almendras, alcaparras y aceitunas.

Rinde unos 5.5 litros

¼ taza de manteca (57g), dividida
½ libra de tomatillos (tomate verde, 2-3 piezas, dependiendo del tamaño)
½ libra de jitomates Roma (jitomate saladet, 1-2 piezas, dependiendo del tamaño), cortados en gajos
Sal, al gusto
1 cebolla blanca pequeña, picada
4 dientes de ajo, machacados
½ libra de almendras (225g), tostadas
½ libra de ajonjolí (225g), tostado
¼ libra más ¼ taza de pasitas, divididas (170g, divididas)
1 ½ cucharaditas (1.5g) de tomillo seco
1 ½ cucharaditas (3g) de granos de pimienta negra
1 ½ cucharaditas (3g) de clavos de olor
1 raja de canela
½ cucharadita (1g) de comino
3 hojas de laurel
1 cucharada sopera (3g) de orégano seco
1 plátano macho, pelado y cortado en trozos de 1 pulgada (2.5 cm)
1 tortilla de maíz, hecha trozos
¼ taza (35g) de alcaparras
¼ taza (40g) de aceitunas verdes picadas
¼ taza (25g) de almendras fileteadas
1 cucharada sopera (12g) de azúcar moreno (o de piloncillo rallado)
¼- ½ taza (60-120 ml) de líquido de escabeche (página 93) o de vinagre blanco destilado, al gusto

1 En una sartén grande o una cacerola de hierro fundido calienta 2 cucharadas soperas de la manteca a fuego medio bajo y cocina los jitomates y los tomatillos a fuego lento por unos 30 minutos, removiendo de vez en cuando hasta que los jitomates se deshagan por completo. Pon sal al gusto. Hazlos puré en una licuadora y devuélvelos a la sartén. Mantén los jitomates a fuego lento para que se reduzcan mientras preparas el resto del mole.

2 Calienta 2 cucharadas soperas más de la manteca en un olla grande y profunda a fuego mediano y saltea la cebolla y el ajo hasta que la cebolla esté transparente, unos 5 minutos.

3 Agrega las almendras tostadas, el ajonjolí, las pasitas, el tomillo, los granos de la pimienta, los clavos de olor, la raja de canela, el comino, el laurel y el orégano a la sartén con la cebolla. Cocina durante unos dos minutos, y a continuación añade el plátano macho y la tortilla. Cocina durante unos 30 minutos; la mezcla se oscurecerá.

4 Trabajando por tandas, combina la mezcla de nueces y semillas con agua suficiente para emulsificarla hasta obtener una pasta suave.

5 Vuelve a colar el puré de nueces en la olla a través de un colador de malla y cuécelo otros 30 a 45 minutos. Seguirá oscureciéndose.

6 Pasa la mezcla de los tomates por el colador e incorporarla a la mezcla de nueces. Remueve bien. Cuece a fuego lento hasta que espese, unos 20 minutos. Pásalo por un colador de malla fina.

7 Agrega al mole las alcaparras, las aceitunas, las pasitas y las almendras fileteadas.

8 Añade las 2 cucharadas soperas de azúcar morena o piloncillo y sal adicional si es necesario. Añade el líquido de escabeche a gusto.

The glass-case figurines, created by Josephina Aguilar, represent residents from different Mexican villages. Tom bought the artworks on his first visit to Oaxaca, even before the restaurant opened. He also requested that the artist represent tourists as part of her growing repertoire. Fran Garcia, Aguilar's grandson, created the six smaller figurines, which depict muxes (moo-shays), also known as third-gender persons. Muxes are recognized and celebrated by the Isthmus Zapotec communities in Oaxaca.

MOLE NEGRO

The complex nature of this pitch-black mole—which boasts 25 ingredients, many of which must be toasted until not quite burnt—means it is often saved for celebratory meals. Most famously, for Día de los Muertos, when it is served with poultry.

Makes about 8 cups

10 chiles chihuacle negro, stems and seeds removed
5 chiles pasilla, stems and seeds removed
1 chile mulato, stem and seeds removed
7 chiles guajillo, stems and seeds removed
2 cups (473mL) water, boiling
1 plantain, peeled
½ white onion, peeled
12 cloves garlic, peeled
¼ pound (115g) Roma tomatoes (1 to 2 tomatoes)
2 tablespoons sesame seeds
10 almonds, whole raw skin-on
10 cashews, whole
2 corn tortillas, torn into pieces
½ bolillo roll, torn into pieces
⅛ teaspoon dried thyme
⅛ teaspoon dried marjoram
¼ cup (40g) raisins
1 tablespoon Mexican oregano
2 quarts (1.9L) water or chicken stock, divided
3 whole cloves
3 whole allspice berries
1 cinnamon stick, broken into pieces
¼ cup (57g) lard
1 ounce (30g, or about ⅓ tablet) Mexican chocolate, such as Abuelita
2 tablespoons sugar
Salt, to taste

1 Toast the chiles in a dry skillet until fragrant, flipping periodically. Use tongs to remove them to a heat-tolerant bowl and cover them with the water.

2 In the same skillet, char the plantain, onion, garlic, and tomatoes, turning them frequently until blackened, about 10 minutes. Put the vegetables in a blender.

3 Toast the sesame seeds until fragrant and add them to the blender.

4 Toast the almonds and cashews until fragrant and add them to the blender. Blend everything until smooth. Add water as needed to help puree.

5 Add the chiles, tortillas, bolillo, thyme, marjoram, raisins, and oregano to the blender and blend until smooth. Add fresh water or chicken stock to help blend.

6 Grind the cloves, allspice, and cinnamon in a spice grinder and add them to the blender. Blend once more, briefly.

7 Heat the lard in a pot over medium heat. Add the mole and remaining water or chicken stock, and simmer for 20 to 30 minutes. (If you're are making the Black Mole Biscuits on page 261, do not thin the paste with liquid.) Add the chocolate and sugar, and stir until the chocolate has melted. Salt to taste.

MOLE NEGRO

La compleja naturaleza de este mole negro azabache, que cuenta con 25 ingredientes, muchos de los cuales deben tostarse hasta casi quemarse hace que tipicamente se reserve para comidas de celebración. El más famoso es el del Día de los Muertos, cuando se sirve con aves.

Rinde 5 litros

10 chilhuacles, sin rabos, venas ni semillas
5 chiles pasilla, sin rabos, venas ni semillas
1 chile mulato, sin rabo, venas ni semillas
7 chiles guajillo, sin rabos, venas ni semillas
2 tazas (473ml) de agua hirviendo
1 plátano macho, sin cascara
Media pieza de cebolla blanca, pelada
12 dientes de ajo, pelados
¼ libra (115g) de jitomate Roma (saladet)
2 cucharadas soperas (18g) de ajonjolí
10 almendras enteras, crudas con la piel
10 nueces de la India
2 tortillas de maíz, hechas trozos
Medio bolillo, hecho trozos
⅛ cucharadita de tomillo seco
⅛ cucharadita de mejorana seca
¼ taza (40 gr) de pasitas
1 cucharada sopera (3g) de orégano mexicano
2 cuartos (1.9L) de agua o caldo de pollo, dividido
3 clavos de olor enteros
3 pimientas gordas enteras
1 raja de canela, hecha trozos
¼ taza (57g) de manteca
1 onza (30 gr) de chocolate mexicano (chocolate de metate de preferencia, o de una marca como Abuelita)
2 cucharadas soperas (25g) de azúcar
Sal, al gusto

1 Tuesta los chiles en un comal o en una sartén seca hasta que estén aromáticos, dándoles la vuelta periódicamente. Utiliza unas pinzas para sacarlos a un bol resistente al calor y cúbrelos con el agua.

2 En el mismo comal o sartén, asa el plátano macho, la cebolla, el ajo y los jitomates, dándoles la vuelta frecuententamenta hasta que se ennegrezcan, unos 10 minutos. Ponga las verduras en una licuadora.

3 Tuesta el ajonjolí hasta que esté aromático y añadirlo a la licuadora.

4 Tuesta las almendras y los nueces de la India hasta que estén aromáticos y añádalos a la licuadora. Licua todo hasta que queda suave. Agrega agua según sea necesario para hacer un puré.

5 Agrega los chiles, las tortillas, el bolillo, el tomillo, la mejorana, las pasitas y el orégano a la licuadora y licua hasta que queda suave. Añade agua o caldo de pollo para ayudar a licuar.

6 Muele los clavos de olor, las pimientas gordas y la canela en un molinillo de especias y agrégalos a la licuadora. Licua una vez más, brevemente.

7 Calienta la manteca en una cacerola a fuego medio. Agrega el mole y el agua o caldo de pollo restantes y cuece a fuego lento de 20 a 30 minutos. (Si estás haciendo los pancitos de la página 261, no diluyes la pasta con el líquido). Agrega el chocolate y el azúcar y remueve hasta que el chocolate se derrita. Sal al gusto.

MOLE VERDE CON VEGETALES

We were inspired by Olga Cabrera while we trained with her in Oaxaca for this recipe, which pairs well with starchy vegetables such as potatoes, corn, zucchini, and even sautéed leafy greens.

Makes about 6 cups

2 serranos, stems removed
1 white onion, peeled and quartered
6 cloves garlic
6 tomatillos, husks removed
2 tablespoons cumin seeds
3 tablespoons dried oregano
10½ cups (2.5L) water, divided
¼ cup (60mL) vegetable oil
6 ounces (170g) fresh white corn masa (page 31)
Salt, to taste
1 bunch cilantro
¼ leaf hoja santa
1 bunch epazote leaves, stems removed

1 Blend the serranos, onion, garlic, tomatillos, cumin, and oregano with 1½ cups water. Puree until smooth.

2 Heat the oil in a large pot over medium-high heat. Carefully pour in the tomatillo liquid and fry it for 2 minutes. Stir the mixture frequently to avoid burning or sticking to the pan.

3 Whisk in 8 cups water.

4 In the blender, add the masa and some of the tomatillo liquid. Blend on high, then season with salt. You want the mixture to coat the back of the spoon.

5 Pass the masa water through a fine mesh strainer into the pot with the tomatillo water.

6 Bring the pot to a boil. Lower it to a simmer, and then cook until thickened and reduced by half, stirring frequently, about 1 hour.

7 Blend the herbs on high with 1 cup water for about 1 minute to liquify, then pass this mixture through a fine mesh strainer into the mole.

8 Bring the mole to a simmer and cook for about 5 minutes. Turn the heat to high to bring it to a rolling boil, then remove from heat. Season to taste and serve warm.

MOLE POBLANO

No shortcuts here. It takes time and patience to develop the layers of flavor in a true Mole Poblano. Miguel Ravago, Fonda San Miguel's founding chef, adapted the restaurant's recipe from one he learned from Diana Kennedy. At the restaurant, it is served with chicken and rice and as a sauce for enchiladas. It is also wonderful on roast turkey and pork.

Makes 2 quarts

4 cups (946mL) water, divided
1 ½ cinnamon stick
3 ½ ounces dried mulato chiles, about 15, stems and veins removed, seeds removed and reserved
1 ½ teaspoons fennel seeds
¾ teaspoon coriander seeds
2 whole cloves
½ teaspoon black peppercorns
10 tablespoons plus ¼ cup (60mL) oil or lard, divided
1 ½ ounces dried pasilla chiles, about 9
2 ounces dried ancho chiles, about 8
2 to 3 quarts chicken stock, as needed
¾ cup (120 g) raisins
2 tablespoons almonds
¼ cup (35g) pepitas
3 6-inch corn tortillas, torn into pieces
8 cloves garlic
6 tomatillos
2 to 3 quarts (1.9 to 2.8L) chicken stock, divided
1 ounce (30g) Mexican chocolate, such as Abuelita, chopped
Salt, to taste

1 Bring a medium-sized pot of water to a boil. Remove from heat.
2 In a dry skillet or cast-iron pan, toast the cinnamon stick, reserved chile seeds, fennel seeds, and coriander seeds over medium until fragrant, about 3 minutes.
3 Remove the spices to a spice grinder and add the cloves and black peppercorns. Grind into a powder, and add to a medium mixing bowl.
4 In the same pan, heat 2 tablespoons oil over medium heat. Fry the chiles for about 15 seconds on each side, until puffed and darkened. Work in batches to make sure they don't burn. Add the chiles to the hot water and let soak for 20 minutes.
5 Heat another 2 tablespoons oil in the pan. Fry the raisins until puffed, about 1 minute, and use a slotted spoon to remove them to the bowl with the spices.
6 Heat 2 tablespoons oil and fry the almonds until fragrant and slightly darkened, about 1 minute. Use a slotted spoon to remove them to the mixing bowl.
7 Heat 2 tablespoons oil and fry the pepitas until they pop, about 2 minutes. Use a slotted spoon to remove them to the mixing bowl.
8 Heat 2 tablespoons oil and fry the tortillas until crisped, about 3 minutes. Use a slotted spoon to remove them to the mixing bowl.
9 Sauté the garlic cloves in whatever oil is left in the pan until golden. Use a slotted spoon to remove them to the mixing bowl.
10 In a small saucepan, cover the tomatillos with water and bring to a boil, then reduce to a simmer. Simmer until softened and darker in color, about 8 minutes.
11 Remove the chiles from the water using a slotted spoon or tongs, and add them to a blender. Add enough chicken stock to cover and puree until smooth. Discard the chile water.
12 Heat ¼ cup oil in a larger heavy-bottomed pot over medium heat. Add the chile mixture, taking caution as it will splatter. Cook the chile sauce for 20 minutes, stirring often to prevent sticking, as it darkens and thickens.
13 Meanwhile, add the contents of the mixing bowl and the tomatillos to a blender and cover with chicken stock (1 quart, or more as needed). Blend until smooth.
14 Add the blender mixture to the chile mixture and cook for 45 minutes, stirring often to prevent scorching.
15 Add the chocolate shards and stir until melted into the sauce. Salt to taste.

Chile Ancho
Adobo Recado
Recado Para Pollo
Chile Negro
Chile de Árbol

RECADOS

Mexican Oregano from Yucatán

Recado Negro

Chile Pasilla

Recado Rojo

RECADO ROJO

Recados are seasoning blends from the Yucatán. Some are available commercially, but at the restaurant, we prefer to make them from scratch.

Makes about 1 cup

3 dried morita chiles, stem and seeds removed
3 dried ancho chiles, stem and seeds removed
2 cups (473mL) water, boiling
2 tablespoons roasted dried garlic
⅔ cup (16g) dried oregano
2 tablespoons salt
1 tablespoon freshly ground black pepper
¾ teaspoon bay leaf powder
¼ cup (30g) chile powder

1 Place chiles in a heat-tolerant bowl and cover with the boiling water. Set aside until cooled.
2 Add cooled chiles to a blender along with remaining ingredients. Add just enough of the chile water so you can blend the ingredients into a paste, 1 to 1 ½ cups. Blend until smooth.

ADOBO DE GUAJILLO, PASILLO, Y ANCHO

Inspired by las Dos Hermanas, page 87, this fiery chile paste has many applications, including Pulpo a la Parilla, page 164, and Rulo de Salmon, page 247.

Makes 1 quart

2 Roma tomatoes
1 cup (240mL) canola oil
6 guajillo chiles, stems, seeds, and veins removed
4 ancho chiles, stems, seeds, and veins removed
2 pasilla chiles, stems, seeds, and veins removed
3 cups (710mL) water, boiling
8 allspice berries
4 whole cloves
1 tablespoon cumin seeds
½ teaspoon whole black peppercorn
1 tablespoon Mexican oregano
5 cloves garlic
½ cup (120mL) apple cider vinegar
2 tablespoons sugar
1 teaspoon salt

1 Heat a large heavy skillet over medium-high heat. Cook the tomatoes, turning frequently, until softened and charred in several places, about 15 minutes. Set aside.
2 Heat oil in the same skillet. Don't allow the oil to smoke.
3 Fry the chiles a few at a time, turning repeatedly until they have darkened, being careful not to burn them. This will take 1 to 2 minutes per batch. Set them aside in a large bowl as you work. Discard the oil, except for about 2 tablespoons.
4 Cover fried chiles with hot water, and allow them to soak for about 20 minutes to soften.
5 While the chiles soak, toast the allspice, cloves, cumin, and peppercorns in a sauté pan on medium heat.
6 Using a molcajete, spice grinder, or blender, grind the toasted spices.
7 Add the chiles to the blender, reserving the water, along with the tomatoes, oregano, garlic, vinegar, sugar, and salt. Blend to a smooth puree, adding chile soaking water as necessary to desired consistency.
8 Heat the skillet over medium heat until hot but not smoking. Add the puree and simmer for 15 minutes. The color will darken once it's ready.

RECADO PARA POLLO

As the name suggests, this Dos Hermanas–inspired seasoning is perfect for chicken and all poultry. It's also fantastic on roasted vegetables.

Makes 1 ½ cups

¼ cup (60g) kosher salt
¼ cup (75g) iodized salt
2 tablespoons ground cumin
2 tablespoons freshly ground black pepper
¾ teaspoon bay leaf powder
1 ½ teaspoons white pepper
¾ teaspoon cinnamon
¼ cup (30g) roasted garlic powder
¼ cup (25g) guajillo powder
2 tablespoons coriander powder

1. Combine all ingredients.
2. Store in an airtight container.

Dos Hermanas

María Elidé Castillo, left, and Delfina Castillo Tzab need no introduction to those eager to attend the next Visiting Chef dinner at Fonda San Miguel. That's because las Dos Hermanas, or the Two Sisters, have made several appearances, with future returns guaranteed. And with good reason: The two women are respected for their multicourse Yucatán feast, featuring their own seeds, curated condiments, and authentic cooking techniques. And their engaging personalities add joy to any gathering.

The Hermanas' success began when the need to earn a living led Elidé, as she prefers to be called, to turn locally sourced foods into spices and ingredients. Her sister joined her in building a business and the women's cooperative Semilla de Dioses, Seed of God. The Castillo sisters also run a cooking school in an intimate setting in Mérida. Star pupils have included Fonda San Miguel chefs, such as former Co-Executive Chef Carlos Monroy. In 2022 the sisters invited him to assist in preparing a multicourse Yucatán feast for members of the exclusive Explorer's Club in New York City.

Whether in their kitchen in Mérida, ours in Austin, or someone else's elsewhere, we welcome the creation and introduction of authentic Yucatán food. *¡Gracias siempre, hermanas Elidé y Delfina!*

RECADO NEGRO

This striking pitch-black recado is made by charring and soaking chiles, and it comes to us from las Dos Hermanas. You'll need to start this at least a day before you plan to use it.

Makes 2 cups

½ ounce (14g, about 40) chiles de árbol, stems removed
3.5 ounces (100g, about 20) guajillo, stems removed
Water to cover
5 stale corn tortillas
1 ½ teaspoons achiote paste
1 ½ teaspoons black peppercorns
½ teaspoon cumin seed
1 ½ teaspoons allspice berries
5 cloves
6 cloves garlic, unpeeled
½ white onion, peeled and quartered
1 habanero chile
1 chipotle chile en adobo
1 tablespoon Mexican oregano
¼ cup (60mL) vinegar, distilled, cider, or banana
1 tablespoon salt

1 Heat oven to 425°F. Arrange the chiles in a large roasting pan, ideally in one layer. Roast until completely black and smoking, about 15 minutes. Turn off the oven but leave the chiles in another 30 minutes.

2 Move the chiles to a large pot. Crush and mash them with a potato masher or large spoon. Cover them with water. Line a strainer with cheesecloth and pour off the water, squeezing out as much water as possible.

3 Put the chiles back in a bowl, and cover them with water again. Use running water to clean your cheesecloth into the bowl, so you catch the bits of chile stuck to it. Change the water twice again, and let the chiles soak overnight. When you drain the water in the morning, reserve the water.

4 The next day, char your tortillas. With gas or electric burners, set them on the burner until they catch fire, blow them out, and flip and char the other side. You can also set them on a very hot cast-iron pan or griddle until you get lots of blackening.

5 Crush the tortillas and put them in a blender along with the achiote paste.

6 Toast the peppercorns, cumin seed, allspice berries, and cloves in a dry pan to bring out aromatics. Grind this in a spice grinder, then add them to the blender.

7 Char the habanero, onion, and garlic in a comal. Add these to the blender.

8 Add the chiles, the chipotles, and the Mexican oregano to the blender. Puree all of this thoroughly, adding reserved soaking water as needed to make the blades run smoothly, 1 to 1 ¼ cups.

9 Strain the recado again with cheesecloth, into a mixing bowl. Squeeze out as much water as you can. Add the vinegar and salt, and stir to combine.

RECADO PARA PUCHERO

Inspired by David Sterling's *Yucatán* cookbook (UT Press), this seasoning blend is typically used in stews.

Makes about ½ cup

3 tablespoons whole coriander seeds
1 tablespoon cumin seeds
1 tablespoon dried oregano
1 teaspoon black peppercorns
1 teaspoon ground cinnamon
1 star anise
¾ teaspoon whole cloves
1 pinch saffron
1 teaspoon achiote paste

1 Pulse together all ingredients minus the achiote paste.
2 Mix in the achiote paste—a little water may help, if needed.

RECADO PARA CARNE

A relatively simple recado that brings mild heat and earthy chile flavors, this recado adds a bit of depth to grilled meats.

Makes about ½ cup

¼ cup (30g) guajillo powder
¼ cup (30g) pasilla powder
1 tablespoon roasted garlic powder
1 tablespoon onion powder
1 teaspoon salt

1 Mix the ingredients together.
2 Store in an airtight container until ready to use.

GARNISHES Y SIDES

ESCABECHE

This combination of pickled vegetables is a welcome addition to an appetizer platter or buffet and also complements grilled meat. Like most pickled dishes, it tastes better after the vegetables have absorbed the pickling brine and the flavors are blended. Refrigerated, it keeps well for two to three weeks.

Makes 1 quart

2 tablespoons olive oil
8 cloves garlic
3 jalapeños, pierced a few times with a knife
12 white pearl onions, peeled
¾ cup (75g) cauliflower florets
2 carrots, peeled and cut into ¼-inch slices
2 small red potatoes, cut in quarters, cooked until tender
¾ cup (80g) fresh green beans, trimmed
Brine, heated
1 teaspoon salt

1 Heat the olive oil in a medium-large saucepan over medium heat. Add the garlic, jalapeños, onions, cauliflower, and carrots. Sauté about 10 minutes, or until softened. Remove from heat.
3 Add vegetables, potatoes, and green beans to a heat-tolerant container. Pour the hot Brine over the top.
4 Season this mixture to taste. Allow to cool completely before serving.

Brine

1 cup (240mL) rice wine vinegar
¾ cup (180mL) water
5 bay leaves
½ teaspoon ground cumin
½ teaspoon whole black peppercorns
½ teaspoon salt
1½ teaspoons dried marjoram
1½ teaspoons Mexican oregano
1 sprig fresh rosemary

1 Add all ingredients to a pot and bring to a full boil.
2 Reduce heat to medium low, and simmer for 15 minutes. Remove from heat. Keep warm until ready to use.

HABANERO RELISH

This fiery condiment can be used as a relish, or the brine can be used on its own to add tang and heat.

Makes about 1 cup

1 cup (240g) rice vinegar
1 teaspoon salt
½ cup (100g) sugar
10 habaneros, stems removed
½ white onion, roughly chopped

1 Bring the vinegar, salt, and sugar to a boil in a small saucepan. Allow the sugar to dissolve, then lower the heat to keep warm until needed.
2 Pulse the habanero and onion in a food processor until minced but not pureed. Add this mixture to a clean jar.
3 Pour the hot vinegar over the habanero mixture, let cool, cover, and store in the refrigerator. This relish is better the day after it's made.

COLIFLOR EN ESCABECHE

Two colors of pickled cauliflower add crunch and acid to tacos and ceviches.

Makes about 6 cups

Purple Cauliflower
3 cups (300g) purple cauliflower, cut into bite-size florets
2 tablespoons pickling spice
½ cup (100g) granulated sugar
1 cup (240mL) red wine vinegar
½ cup (120mL) water
½ teaspoon salt

Yellow Cauliflower
3 cups (300g) yellow cauliflower, cut into bite-size florets
2 tablespoons pickling spice
½ cup (100g) granulated sugar
1 cup (240mL) rice wine vinegar
½ cup (120mL) water
½ teaspoon salt
½ teaspoon turmeric

1 Place cauliflower in a quart jar.
2 In a small pot, bring the pickling spice, sugar, vinegar, salt, and water (and turmeric for yellow cauliflower pickles) to a boil.
3 Pour pickling liquid over the florets so they are fully immersed. Add a weight to keep the florets down.
4 Allow the jar to cool to room temperature, then store the pickled cauliflower in the liquid, in the refrigerator.

CEBOLLAS EN ESCABECHE

These bright red onion slices are a traditional garnish for Cochinita Pibil on page 106, nice to have on hand for serving grilled or barbecued meats. The fresh beet added to the marinade increases the brilliance of color and adds a touch of sweetness, but they can be left out if you prefer.

Makes 2 to 3 cups

1 large red onion, thinly sliced
12 whole black peppercorns
3 cloves garlic, thinly sliced
1 red beet, quartered
1 cup (240g) red wine vinegar
½ teaspoon salt

1 Combine all ingredients in a large mixing bowl and allow to pickle at room temperature for 2 hours, stirring occasionally.
2 Remove the beets and discard.
3 These are best served at room temperature, but store them in the refrigerator, undrained, for up to several days until ready to serve.

PEPITAS DULCES

Careful: These sweet and spicy roasted pumpkin seeds are addictive. We use them as garnishes on soups, salads, vegetables dishes—and just as a snack, by the handful.

Makes 1 cup

1 teaspoon oil
½ cup (120mL) water
¼ cup (50g) sugar
1 cup (140g) pepitas, roasted
1 tablespoon plus 2 teaspoons (12g) chile de árbol powder, divided
½ teaspoon kosher salt

1 Heat oven to 375°F.
2 Line a cookie sheet with parchment paper and lightly oil.
3 In a small pot, add the water and sugar, and heat over medium heat until the sugar dissolves.
4 Add the pepitas, 1 tablespoon chile de árbol powder, and salt to the syrup. Bring this to a boil, then reduce it to a simmer, stirring occasionally, until most of the liquid is gone, about 10 minutes.
5 Use a rubber spatula to spread the pepitas evenly over the prepared sheet pan.
6 Bake the pepitas for 5 to 8 minutes, until crisped and browned. Once you remove them from the oven, sprinkle them with 2 teaspoons chile de árbol powder and allow to cool.
7 Break the pepitas apart and store in an airtight container at room temperature.

Muchacha con Limones. Francisco Zuñiga.

Top: *Mujer con Pescados*. Bottom: *Ninas con Panes*.
Both Francisco Zuñiga.

Top: *La Comida*. Bottom: *La Fonda*.
Both Francisco Zuñiga.

Diablito Violeta Cazador. Teodulo Romulo.

Opposite top: *Girl with Butterfly*. Cuban artist.
Opposite bottom: *Woman with Blue Flower*. Cuban artist.
Above: *Brujas*. Master Marenal.

Dos Pajaros. Teodulo Romulo.

RAJAS Y CEBOLLAS

These strips of roasted poblano chiles and onions are a functional side dish or condiment for grilled meats and many other dishes. They beautifully garnish all kinds of tacos and are a simple but delicious filling for tamales.

Makes about 3 cups

3 large poblano peppers
3 tablespoons vegetable oil, divided
1 large white onion, thinly sliced
Salt, to taste

1 Heat oven to 400°F.
2 Toss the poblanos in 1 ½ tablespoons oil and roast them on a sheet pan for 10 minutes.
3 Place the roasted chiles in a heat-tolerant bowl and immediately cover with plastic wrap. Let sit for about 15 minutes.
4 Once cool enough to handle, remove the skin and seeds of the poblanos and discard them.
5 Thinly slice the poblanos the full length of the chile.
6 In a sauté pan, heat 1 ½ tablespoons oil over medium heat. Sauté the onions until transparent, about 10 minutes. Add the poblanos and sauté another 5 minutes. Add salt as desired.

FRIJOLES REFRITOS

Refried beans make a rich and creamy companion for many entrees, especially when they are enhanced with a dollop of sour cream and a sprinkling of crumbled panela cheese. They are also a tasty topping for nachos and sopes. If you are making a recipe that calls for whole beans, simply follow step one and drain.

Makes about 3 cups

1 cup (200g) dried pinto beans
Water, enough to cover
10 leaves fresh epazote
3 tablespoons lard or shortening
3 cloves garlic, smashed
1 onion, diced
2 chipotle chiles en adobo
Salt, to taste

1 In a large pot, cover the beans with plenty of water and add the epazote. Bring this to a boil, then reduce it to a simmer. Cook, uncovered, until the beans are tender—it's better to overcook than undercook them here. Depending on the age of your dried beans, this can take anywhere from 1 hour to several hours. Top off the water if the beans become uncovered.
2 While the beans are cooking, heat the lard in a sauté pan over medium heat. Add the garlic and the onions and cook until the onions are translucent, about 5 minutes.
3 Puree the onion mixture along with the chipotle in a blender until smooth. Salt to taste.
4 Drain the beans, reserving 2 cups of the cooking liquid. Combine the drained beans and the onion puree in a large sauté pan over medium-low heat. Cook, stirring and mashing with the back of a spoon, until beans are thickened to a paste. Taste and add salt as desired. You may also use the cooking liquid to thin the beans to your desired consistency.

ARROZ BLANCO

Mexican dishes are served with a wide range of rice dishes, from red to green and even black, colored with squid ink. Many coastal seafood dishes are served with a white rice, like this. The peas here add a splash of color.

Makes 8 servings

¼ cup (60mL) canola oil
2 cups (370g) long grain rice
4 cups (960mL) chicken broth or water
1 cup (150g) frozen peas, thawed
1 teaspoon salt

1 Heat the oil in a heavy 3-quart sauce pan over medium-high heat.
2 Add the rice and cook, stirring, for about 8 minutes, or until the rice is golden.
3 Add the chicken broth, bring to a boil, reduce to a simmer, cover, and cook for 20 minutes, or until the liquid has been absorbed.
4 Fluff with a fork, add peas, and season with salt.

CALDO DE POLLO BÁSICO

This is Chef Miguel's all-purpose stock recipe. It is a rich, flavorful foundation on which many other recipes are built. Although time-consuming to make, it will add depth of flavor to any recipe that calls for chicken broth or stock. The smartest thing to do is make it in large batches and freeze quart portions for future use.

Makes 2 quarts

1 whole frying chicken, cut up
1 medium white onion, sliced
1 carrot, sliced
3 cloves garlic, mashed
8 whole black peppercorns
1 teaspoon sea salt
Water to cover

1 Combine all ingredients in an 8-quart stock pot with water, and bring to a simmer over medium heat.
2 Cook 35 to 45 minutes, or until chicken is tender. With a slotted spoon, remove chicken pieces and allow to cool.
3 Remove the meat from the bones and refrigerate for another use.
4 Return the bones to the broth and cook 1 hour.
5 Remove from heat and allow to cool to room temperature. Refrigerate until fat solidifies on the surface, 6 to 8 hours.
6 Using a slotted spoon or skimmer, skim off fat from the surface of the stock. Strain stock before using.

Fonda San Miguel

Section Two

A FRESH START

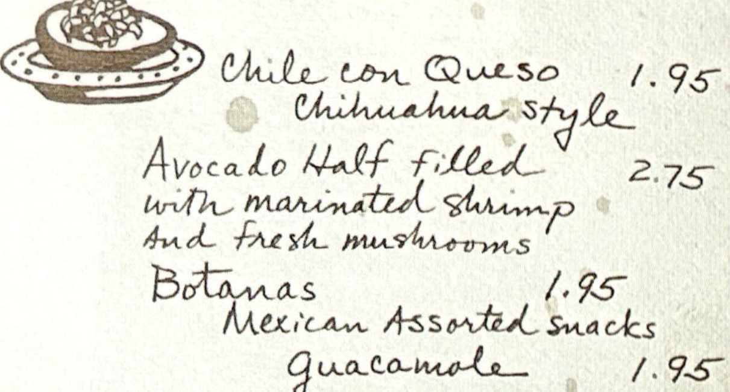

Chile con Queso 1.95
Chihuahua style

Avocado Half filled 2.75
with marinated shrimp
And fresh mushrooms

Botanas 1.95
Mexican Assorted snacks

Guacamole 1.95

Mexican Tortilla Soup 1.25

Mexican Corn Soup 1.25

Mixed Green Salad .85

Poblano Chile stuffed 2.75
with guacamole
(in season)

Pollo Pibil 3.75
chicken seasoned Yucatan
style & cooked in A
banana leaf

Cornish Game Hen en Mole Poblano 4.95
San Miguel prepares
its own Mole from
The traditional Puebla recipe

15% Gratuity Added for 6 or more

Fonda San Miguel takes great care in using The correct And finest ingredients in presenting The truly classical cooking of Mexico.

A partial shopping List:

Fresh Chiles
Serrano, Poblano, Anaheim & Jalapeño

Dry Chiles
Ancho, Guajillo, Mulatto, Pasilla And Chipótle

Spices
Achiote, Anise, Cinammon, Comino, Sesame & pépitas

Herbs
Epazote, Oregano, Cilantro

Miscellaneous
Acitron, Almonds, banana leaves & Tomatillos

For Those interested in The Art of classical Mexican Cooking As found in Mexico And At Fonda San Miguel, we highly recommend

The Cuisines of Mexico
And
The Tortilla Book
by
Diana Kennedy

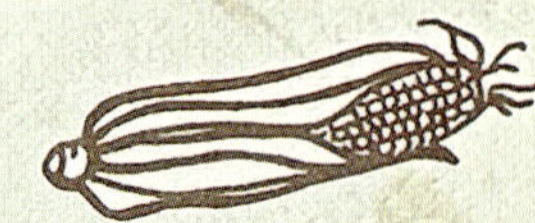

2330 W. North Loop, Austin 459-4121

SOPA DE TORTILLA

This is a simple old-fashioned version of tortilla soup that's been on the Fonda San Miguel menu since the seventies. The soup is cooked until tortillas break down in the broth, giving it texture, flavor, and body. It's then garnished with—what else?—more strips of crunchy tortilla.

Serves 4 to 6

¼ cup (55g) plus 2 tablespoons lard or oil, divided
7 corn tortillas, divided into 5 tortillas and 2 tortillas, and cut into strips
6 Roma tomatoes
1 white onion, roughly chopped
4 cloves garlic
3 quarts (2.8L) chicken stock
10 epazote leaves
1 cup (100g) shredded Monterey Jack cheese
5 chile pasillas, toasted and crumbled
Salt, to taste

1 Heat ¼ cup lard in skillet until shimmering. Fry strips from 5 tortillas until golden, about 10 minutes, then remove with a slotted spoon to a paper-towel lined plate. Repeat with remaining strips, for garnish.

2 In a dry skillet or cast-iron pan, cook the tomatoes until softened and blackened in places, 7 to 10 minutes.

3 Add tomato with onion and garlic to a blender, and puree until smooth.

4 In a large heavy-bottomed pot, heat 2 tablespoons lard almost to smoking over medium-high heat. Add the puree and simmer, stirring frequently, until it reduces and turns dark red, about 30 minutes. Caution: The puree will splatter when it hits the hot oil.

5 Add the chicken stock and bring it to a boil.

6 Add the larger pile of tortilla strips and the epazote leaves to the pot. Simmer until the tortillas dissolve, about 1 hour. Season to taste.

7 To serve, in a bowl add a small amount of cheese, a few tortilla strips, and a pinch of crumbled pasilla, and ladle in the soup.

Tom's cursive handwriting and basic sketches provided the restaurant's first menu (1975). Since then, the menus and wine lists have featured designs by well-known artists, including Arnulfo Mendoza, Sergio Bustamante, and Pedro Friedeberg, whose hand-shaped wooden chair is on display in the restaurant.

COCHINITA PIBIL

Cochinita Pibil is the traditional pork barbecue of the Yucatán Peninsula, where for centuries it has been cooked in pits lined with hot stones and banana leaves. The achiote-based rub, which imparts a rich terracotta color and an earthy flavor, is equally good on seafood and Pollo Pibil Yucatán, on page 115.

Serves 6

4 pounds (1.8kg) pork shoulder or butt, trimmed of tendons and cut into 2.5-inch cubes
2 tablespoons safflower oil
4 large tomatoes, sliced
2 medium white onions, sliced
2 tablespoons reserved Achiote Rub
1 large banana leaf
Cebollas en Escabeche (page 95)
Arroz Blanco (page 99)

Achiote Rub

2 tablespoons achiote seeds or 3 tablespoons achiote paste
¼ cup (60mL) orange juice
½ cup (120mL) distilled white vinegar
½ teaspoon cumin seeds
½ teaspoon dried Mexican oregano
12 whole black peppercorns
4 whole allspice berries
8 cloves garlic
¼ teaspoon paprika
1 tablespoon sea salt

Note

If using prepared achiote paste instead of achiote seeds, skip the soaking and crushing steps. Simply mash the paste with the orange juice and vinegar and then transfer the mixture to a blender.

1 Prepare the Achiote Rub. Mix the achiote seeds with the orange juice and vinegar, and soak 1 hour to soften them.
2 Using a molcajete, or mortar and pestle, crush the achiote seeds with a little of the soaking liquid.
3 Transfer the seeds and soaking liquid to a blender and add the remaining rub ingredients; blend to a paste.
4 Reserve 2 tablespoons for cooking with the tomatoes.
5 Rub the pork cubes with the Achiote Rub and set aside.
6 Heat oil in a heavy skillet over medium heat.
7 Add tomatoes, onions, and the reserved 2 tablespoons of Achiote Rub. Fry for about 3 minutes and set aside.
8 Preheat oven to 350°F. Have a large, heavy Dutch oven ready.
9 Using tongs, carefully sear the banana leaf over an open flame until flexible.
10 Line the Dutch oven with the banana leaf and arrange the pork cubes on the leaf.
11 Cover the pork with the tomato mixture, folding the banana leaf over the top.
12 Cover and cook for 2 to 2½ hours, basting occasionally with juices from the bottom of the pot.
13 Remove from the oven and transfer to a serving platter.
14 Garnish with Cebollas Rojas en Escabeche and serve with Arroz Blanco.

Variation

Substitute 4 pounds chicken pieces for the pork. Brown in a skillet with a little oil. Proceed as directed.

In 1994 Fonda San Miguel was the first Texas restaurant invited to the prestigious James Beard House, in New York City, where Chef Miguel Ravago (center top) and his team created the renowned Sunday Buffet for appreciative diners. They did some prep around the corner at Bobby Flay's Mesa Grill. Pictured with Ravago are Flay's pastry chef at the time (left), Diana Kennedy, and Tom Gilliland.

Ingredientes para 6 porciones

4 libras (1.8kg) de espaldilla de puerco sin tendones, y cortado en cubitos de 2.5 pulgadas (6-6.5 cm)
2 cucharadas soperas (30ml) de aceite de cártamo
4 jitomates grandes (800g), cortados en rodajas
2 cebollas blancas medianas (300g), cortadas en rodajas
2 cucharadas soperas del Aliño de Achiote reservadas
1 hoja de plátano grande
Cebollas en Escabeche (página 95)
Arroz Blanco (página 99)

Aliño de Achiote

2 cucharadas soperas de achiote o
 3 cucharadas soperas de pasta de achiote
¼ taza (60ml) de jugo de naranja
½ taza (120ml) de vinagre blanca destilada
½ cucharadita de comino
½ cucharadita de orégano mexicano
12 granos de pimienta negra enteras
4 granos de pimienta gorda
8 dientes de ajo, pelados
¼ cucharadita de pimentón
1 cucharada sopera de sal marina

Nota

Si usas la pasta de achiote preparada en lugar de las semillas, omite los pasos de remojo y machacado. Simplemente combina el jugo de naranja y el vinagre y a continuación, transfiera la mezcla a una licuadora.

1 Prepara el Aliño de Achiote. Mezcla las semillas de achiote con el jugo de naranja y el vinagre y déjalas en remojo durante una hora para que se ablanden.

2 Utilizando un molcajete o un mortero, machaca las semillas con un poco del líquido de remojo.

3 Pasa las semillas a una licuadora y añade los ingredientes restantes para el aliño; licua hasta obtener una pasta.

4 Reserva 2 cucharadas soperas de la pasta para cocinar con los jitomates.

5 Frota los cubitos de cerdo con el Aliño de Achiote y resérvalos.

6 Calienta el aceite en un sartén grueso a fuego medio.

7 Agrega los jitomates, la cebolla y las 2 cucharadas soperas del Aliño de Achiote reservadas. Fríe durante unos 3 minutos y reserva.

8 Precalentar el horno a 350 grados F (180 C). Ten preparada una cacerola grande y gruesa.

9 Utiliza unas pinzas para pasar la hoja de plátano cuidadosamente por encima de una llama abierta hasta que esté flexible.

10 Forra la cacerola con las hoja de plátano y coloca los cubitos de puerco encima de la hoja.

11 Cubra la carne de cerdo con la mezcla de jitomate, doblando la hoja de plátano por encima.

12 Tapa y cuece en el horno precalentado de 2 a 2.5 horas, rociando de vez en cuando con los jugos del fondo de la cacerola.

13 Retira del horno y pásalo a un plato para servir.

14 Adorna con las Cebollas en Escabeche y sirve con el Arroz Blanco.

Variación

Sustituye la carne de puerco por 4 libras de piezas de pollo. Dóralos en una sartén con un poco de aceite. Procede como se indica.

The "Mick Jagger of Mexican Cuisine"

DIANA KENNEDY

The photograph of a woman in a kitchen somewhere—the date and location are unimportant—is the image of an unglamourous celebrity among celebrities. She holds one hand up in the air as if posing, like a dancer. The mischievous twinkle in her eyes conveys she is not an ordinary cook. Nothing about her is ordinary.

The woman is the British food writer Diana Kennedy. DK, as many of her closest friends call her, is credited with inspiring many of the recipes at Fonda San Miguel restaurant. She once described herself as the Mick Jagger of Mexican cuisine. That self-comparison, along with credit for her culinary contributions to Fonda San Miguel, are printed on the restaurant menu, and her framed photo hangs in a place of honor in the restaurant. And with good reason.

Kennedy is recognized as an authority on Mexican cuisine. Her nine cookbooks feature recipes with spices, plants, and cooking techniques from every region of Mexico. Even while she lived and traveled throughout Mexico, she visited Austin often and spent time with Fonda San Miguel co-founders and partners Tom Gilliland and the late chef Miguel Ravago. They were among her closest friends, and the restaurant became her home away from home, where she was resident consultant.

"She took it seriously," says Soll Sussman, who first met Kennedy in 1982, while he was a journalist in Mexico. "She wanted to be sure everything was being prepared authentically. She admired Tom's efforts to keep the food and ambiance of the restaurant authentic. At the time, she was an outspoken environmental activist whose home, Rancho Quintana, was built completely with sustainability in mind."

"A firecracker" is how another close friend, Matt Weissler, describes Kennedy. "She would tell people exactly what she thought," he says, with a laugh. "And not in the most delicate way." A buyer for bookstores, Weissler met Kennedy through Tom and Miguel in the early nineties, when she was a featured author at the Texas Book Festival. After a day of public speaking and book signing, they all retreated to the restaurant, where Weissler says he returned every night for a decade. He also spent the last several years of Kennedy's life as her personal driver and companion, until her death at age 99, in July 2022. "I miss the conversations with her," he says, "talking to her almost daily about small things in life and her observations of nature. I miss being in her yard in Mexico, where she grew her own coffee, which was the best brew in the world."

Sussman recalls wanting to host a party for her ninetieth birthday, but she said no to the idea. Then, for her ninety-fifth, she said, "I'm not a party girl, but when I turn one hundred, you can give me a party!" She would be touched that so many people turned out for her centennial birthday. Both Weissler and Sussman were among the hundreds of guests who gathered at Fonda San Miguel for Diana Kennedy's Centennial Birthday Celebration, on March 5, 2023, two days after her birthday. The gathering featured dishes made from her own recipes, found in her cookbooks and on the Fonda San Miguel menu. Proceeds from the event made it possible to establish an endowment dedicated to preserving her personal collection of cookbooks, now housed at the University of Texas at San Antonio.

Kennedy's commitment to a lifetime of learning about authentic Mexican cuisine continues through scholarships established by Fonda San Miguel for two students enrolled in the Austin Community College District Culinary Arts Program. The scholarships are named in honor of Diana Kennedy and Miguel Ravago.

"When Miguel arrived here, in 1972, he was the first chef to introduce true interior Mexican food to Austin," says Tom Gilliland. "Naming the scholarships after Diana and Miguel continues their legacies of sharing knowledge and elevating authentic Mexican food to its deserved place at the top of culinary achievements. It is just the start of supporting future leaders in the culinary world and building Austin's reputation as a national culinary destination."

Diana Kennedy's life and dedication continue to profoundly impact Fonda San Miguel. A centennial birthday celebration and fundraiser in her honor, held March 5, 2023, led to the establishment of an endowment to preserve her personal collection of cookbooks, housed at the University of Texas at San Antonio.

THIS PAGE CLOCKWISE FROM TOP: Guests await the opening of Fonda San Miguel's doors for the celebration; Diana Kennedy's friends Amalia Rodriguez-Mendoza and Soll Sussman; former executive chef Blanca Zesati, left, Mexic-Arte Museum executive director Sylvia Orozco, and media consultant Olga Campos Benz.

Diana Kennedy lives on through her many friends and those who continue her efforts to elevate authentic Mexican cuisine within the culinary world.

THIS PAGE CLOCKWISE FROM TOP: University of Texas at San Antonio library staff members displaying items from Kennedy's collection of cookbooks; former office manager Janice Harris, left, Tom Gilliland, and Diana Kennedy; Diana Kennedy, left, with filmmaker Robert Rodriguez and Tom Gilliland; Austin Community College Culinary Arts students Jacob Pham and Nicolle Rivera Martinez, recipients of the Miguel Ravago and Diana Kennedy Scholarships.

CAMARONES CHIPOTLE

This recipe, created by former Fonda San Miguel chef Roberto Santibañez, is one of the restaurant's signatures and one of its easiest dishes to recreate at home. Serve it with Arroz Blanco, on page 99.

Serves 4

2 cups (480mL) heavy cream
4 chipotles en adobo
24 large shrimp, peeled and deveined, tail on
Salt, to taste
Black pepper, to taste
2 tablespoons canola oil
¼ cup (60g) finely diced white onion
1 tablespoon minced garlic
1 cup (180g) finely diced Roma tomatoes (1 to 2 tomatoes)
White pepper, to taste

1 In a blender, puree the cream with the chipotles. (Be careful not to overblend and make butter!)

2 Season the shrimp with a large pinch of salt and a few grinds of black pepper. Heat the oil in a large sauté pan over medium-high heat and sauté shrimp briefly, 1 to 2 minutes. The shrimp will not be cooked through entirely.

3 Add the onion, garlic, and tomatoes to the pan. Sauté about 3 minutes.

4 Add the heavy cream mixture and reduce by half to thicken, about 5 minutes. Adjust seasonings and serve.

Caroline Matthews

"I discovered the restaurant years before I had the pleasure of meeting Tom," recalls Caroline Matthews. She first read about Fonda San Miguel in *Texas Monthly* magazine and was so intrigued by the description of its culinary authenticity that she made a special trip from San Antonio just to dine there. The trip was worth it as she devoured every single morsel.

A longtime admirer of the restaurant and its commitment to authenticity, Caroline is also a vendor who has created guayabera for Tom since both were first starting out, he with Fonda San Miguel and she with her company, Dos Carolinas. She fondly recalls the excitement in the early days of finding interesting fabrics to suit Tom's aesthetics.

"I admire Tom for his taste and for his success building a restaurant that is considered to be iconic by anyone's standards," she says. "It's not easy to keep something going, let alone be successful for fifty years! It takes passion. I know. I've been designing and selling custom guayaberas for nearly as long." Whether it's guayaberas or comida, it appears Mexican authenticity and passion pay off.

CUSTOMER FAVORITE
FONDA SAN MIGUEL

POLLO PIBIL YUCATÁN

A faster, lighter preparation than the pork version on page 106, Pollo Pibil Yucatán is nonetheless flavorful and useful in a variety of preparations.

Serves 4 to 6

3 cloves garlic
½ white onion, peeled and quartered
2 tablespoons canola oil
1 ½ teaspoons achiote paste
1 cup (240mL) bitter orange juice
1 cup (240mL) chicken stock
½ teaspoon dried oregano
¼ teaspoon ground cumin
¼ teaspoon ground allspice
1 teaspoon kosher salt
1 teaspoon freshly ground black pepper
1 whole chicken, about 5 pounds, cut into 8 pieces
8 banana leaves

1 Heat oven to 400°F.

2 Wrap the garlic cloves and onion quarters in foil, along with the oil. Set this packet on a small sheet pan (to catch any leaking oil) and roast for about 45 minutes. Let cool completely.

3 Puree the garlic, onions, oil, achiote paste, bitter orange juice, chicken stock, oregano, cumin, allspice, salt, and black pepper in a blender until smooth.

4 Add the chicken pieces to a bowl and pour the marinade over them. Stir to coat, then cover the bowl and refrigerate at least 1 hour and up to overnight.

5 Heat oven to 350°F.

6 To prepare a Dutch oven, microwave banana leaves for about 30 seconds each (if you have sections of banana leaves they will require less time, about 10 seconds) to make them more pliable. Line the Dutch oven with about 6 leaves, overlapping and completely lining the pan. Add the chicken and its marinade, then cover completely with additional banana leaves.

7 Cover the Dutch oven and cook for 1 ½ to 2 hours; the chicken is done when it's falling apart. Remove the Dutch oven from the oven and let steam, covered, for another 15 minutes or so.

8 Use forks or tongs to pull the chicken. Discard bones and combine the pulled chicken with the marinade. Serve warm.

ENCHILADAS SUIZAS DE JAIBA

We serve these distinctive enchiladas around Easter at the restaurant, with a sour cream sauce that won't overwhelm the flavorful crab mixture. The filling in this recipe can also be used for quesadillas or as a topping for sopes.

Makes 12 enchiladas; serves 6 to 8

6 tablespoons vegetable oil
12 corn tortillas
Crabmeat Filling
Sour Cream Sauce

Crabmeat Filling

Makes 3 cups

1 ¼ pounds (565g) lump crabmeat
6 tablespoons olive oil (plus ½ cup for tortillas)
3 tablespoons butter
3 cloves garlic, chopped
1 medium white onion, chopped
2 pickled jalapeños, chopped,
with ¼ cup (60mL) juice from the can
2 or 3 pickled carrots, chopped
2 medium tomatoes, seeded and chopped
¼ cup (15g) chopped fresh parsley
¼ cup (15g) chopped fresh cilantro
Sea salt and ground black pepper to taste

Sour Cream Sauce

Makes 3 ¾ cups

3 cups (720mL) sour cream
¾ cup (180mL) milk
1 teaspoon sea salt
1 teaspoon ground white pepper

1 Prepare the Crabmeat Filling. Pick through the crabmeat and remove bits of shell or cartilage, taking care not to break up the lumps. In a heavy nonreactive skillet, heat the olive oil and butter over medium heat, add garlic and onion, and sauté until the onion is transparent. Add the jalapeños and juice, carrots, tomatoes, parsley, and cilantro and cook for about 3 minutes; season to taste with salt and pepper. Reduce heat to low and cook until mixture thickens, about 20 minutes. Add crabmeat and cook just until crabmeat is heated through. Adjust seasonings as needed. Keep warm.

2 Prepare Sour Cream Sauce. Whisk the ingredients together in a small bowl and set aside.

3 In a small skillet, heat vegetable oil over medium-high heat. Once the oil is hot, use tongs to dip each tortilla in the oil for about 30 seconds to soften, not to make them crispy like chips.

4 Place 3 tablespoons Crabmeat Filling down the center of each tortilla and roll it up. Arrange the enchiladas on an ovenproof serving platter or baking dish. Top with Sour Cream Sauce, place under a broiler for 3 minutes, and serve immediately.

Variation

Stir together one half recipe Salsa Verde de Mesa (page 57) and one half recipe Sour Cream Sauce. After softening tortillas in oil, dip in the warm sauce mixture and fill with Crabmeat Filling as directed above. Cover with a generous serving of the sauce mixture.

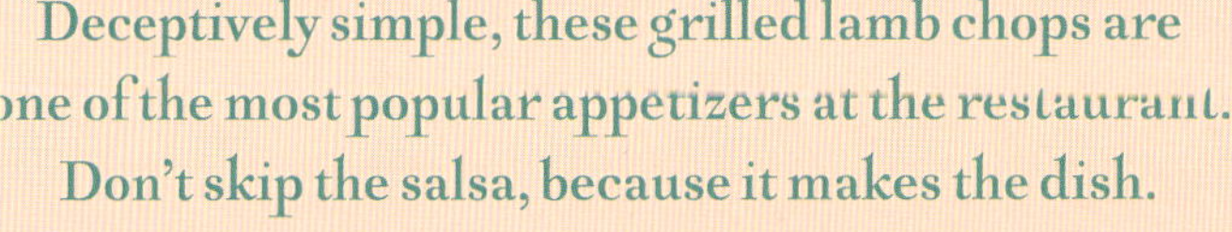

LAMB LOLLIPOPS

Deceptively simple, these grilled lamb chops are one of the most popular appetizers at the restaurant. Don't skip the salsa, because it makes the dish.

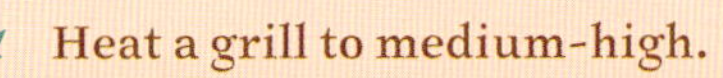

Makes 12 baby chops; serves 6

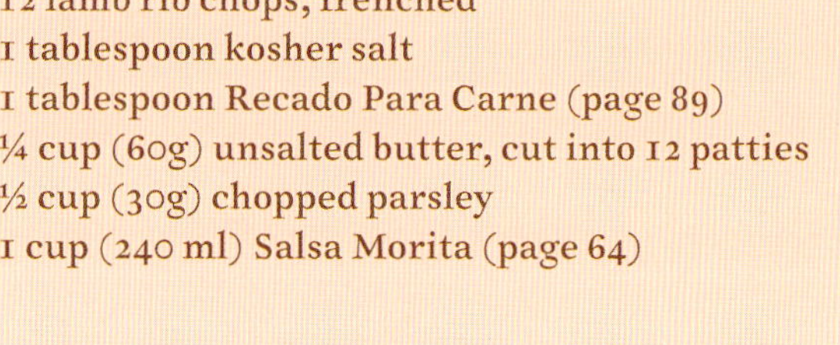

12 lamb rib chops, frenched
1 tablespoon kosher salt
1 tablespoon Recado Para Carne (page 89)
¼ cup (60g) unsalted butter, cut into 12 patties
½ cup (30g) chopped parsley
1 cup (240 ml) Salsa Morita (page 64)

1 Heat a grill to medium-high.

2 Pat chops dry and season with salt on both sides. Then season with Recado Para Carne.

3 Cook chops on the grill for about 2 minutes per side, or until they reach an internal temperature of 135°F. You want these beautifully seared.

4 Remove from grill, and plate each with a small patty of butter on top.

5 Sprinkle with chopped parsley and serve with a small side of Salsa Morita.

An early 1980s luncheon menu features a stylized version of Fagan, Fonda San Miguel's first parrot. Fagan's successor, Paco (below), is in his mid-forties.

FONDA SAN MIGUEL

Luncheon Menu

Karen Frost and Charlie Levy

Love at First Bite!

Karen Frost had given up on dating until fate intervened on New Year's Eve 2008, when she was invited to a party and encouraged to write down qualities she looked for in a life partner. Her list was then transferred to a helium balloon and ceremoniously released into the universe. Happy New Year!

At the time, Karen's work as a public relations rep kept her traveling year-round. "Often my trips ended with a stop at Fonda San Miguel. Tom became a friend and a client," she recalls.

Not long after wading back into the dating pool, Karen connected with Charlie Levy, and he agreed to meet her at Fonda San Miguel, where Tom was hosting his seventieth birthday party.

Charlie describes Karen's invitation as more of a first look than a first date. "I almost backed out," he says. "I'd never been to Fonda San Miguel, and it was raining." Fate nudged him, and boy, was he glad he went. He spotted a gorgeous Karen, who was busy talking to other guests, leaving him free to dive into the Fonda feast.

"Those were the best lambchops I had ever tasted. And the bacon-wrapped shrimp are amazing. I fell in love at first bite!" he jokes. "Or was it love at first sight?" Likely it was both.

Karen finally took a break from schmoozing and suggested Charlie join her at a table to talk. That was followed by lunch the next day, followed by time together every day for the next six months. Seven love-filled years later they were married.

For the couple, Tom Gilliland's birthday on January 23, 2008, will always be a night of "firsts," which they continue to celebrate annually at their special table, where lollipop lambchops, bacon-wrapped shrimp, and love still sizzle.

Charlie Levy and Karen Frost

PESCADO A LA PLANCHA

This simple preparation of grilled fish is another Fonda San Miguel classic! Seasoned with Recado Rojo, it is best served with Arroz Blanco, Salsa Verde de Mesa, and Rajas y Cebollas.

Serves 4

2 tablespoons canola oil
4 skinless black drum filets, about ½ pound (230g) each
Salt, to taste
¼ cup (30g) Recado Rojo (page 86)
Salsa Verde de Mesa (page 57), for serving
Arroz Blanco (page 99), for serving
Rajas y Cebollas, warmed (page 98), for serving

1. In a skillet, heat the oil over medium-high heat.
2. Season each filet all over with a generous pinch of salt and 1 tablespoon Recado Rojo.
3. Sear the drum about 3 minutes flesh-side down, and carefully flip over and cook another 2 minutes.
4. Serve with suggested side dishes immediately.

Janice Harris

"Fonda San Miguel is like a clock that keeps going, even through struggles and setbacks, as all restaurants experience," says Janice Harris, pictured with Miguel Ravago. "Yet Fonda keeps evolving and maintaining high standards."

Janice knows, because she worked as office manager at the restaurant for 30 years. Some "aspects" of the job she misses dearly: "The margaritas, the Pescado al Mojo de Ajo, the Conchinita Pibil, the Enchiladas Suizas..."

Strong customer relationships were a joy for her too, she says. As office manager, Janice was present to accept payment for large groups, such as the exclusive crew wrap party for the movie *Courage Under Fire*, after it completed filming outside Austin in the nineties. "It was the thrill of my life to sit next to Academy Award winner Denzel Washington," she says, "as he wrote out a check to pay for the entire event!"

She knows Fonda San Miguel has not missed a beat remaining true to its authentic cuisine "just like the day it opened," and she wishes for 50 more years of those high standards.

TINGA DE POLLO

Everyone needs a simple Chicken Tinga recipe in their pocket, for use in enchiladas, tacos, quesadillas, sopes, and more. And this is ours! You can substitute chicken thighs for the breasts, if you prefer.

Makes 3 cups (fills 12 enchiladas)

¼ cup (40g) chopped, white onion
2 cloves garlic, chopped
4 medium tomatoes, roasted and chopped
3 chipotle chiles in adobo sauce
2 tablespoons adobo sauce from the can
2 to 3 boneless chicken breasts, poached in water, seasoned with sea salt and ground black pepper, then cooked and shredded (about 2 cups)
⅓ cup (80mL) chicken broth, reserved from cooking chicken
Sea salt and ground black pepper, to taste

1 Cook onion and garlic over low heat, stirring constantly, until onions are transparent.
2 Add tomatoes, chiles, and adobe sauce. Increase heat to medium and cook, stirring often, until all moisture has been absorbed and the mixture is dry, about 15 minutes.
3 Stir in shredded poached chicken and broth. Cook another 3 to 4 minutes, until chicken is heated through.
4 Season to taste with salt and pepper.

Edgar Yepez-Garcia

Folklórico dancer

Edgar Yepez-Garcia may have earned a computer science degree and worked as a radio host, but his life's calling is to dance and share the joy and beauty of that performance art with others. He started dancing at age six in Oaxaca, Mexico, where he was born and raised. He was a member of the Ballet Folklórico Tochtepetl and, as a dancer, traveled throughout Mexico and Central America before landing in 2007 in Austin, where he founded Ballet Folklórico de Austin.

Edgar is among the many close friends of the restaurant who have been intimately involved with its operations. "I will treasure the time I worked in Fonda San Miguel as the kitchen manager," he says. "I learned from the best people, and I had the opportunity to know the inside of the amazing FSM world."

When Edgar organized the first ever Guelaguetza Austin, the traditional festival to celebrate the music, dance, food, and drink of Oaxaca, Fonda San Miguel helped financially. "Tom and FSM have supported our cultural idea since our first meeting," says Edgar. "I remember Tom expressed all the love he has for Mexico and all our traditions. We bought our Tehuanas dresses with a generous donation from Tom and Fonda San Miguel." Edgar is grateful to feature the restaurant as a beautiful complementary backdrop to his costumed dancers over the years.

"I see Fonda San Miguel as more than a culinary institution in Austin," says Edgar. "It brings the very best of Mexico to our eyes. Not just the food, but the music, art, language, and dance. And most importantly, our people. Few restaurants, if any, can adequately deliver the magnificence of Mexico, but Fonda San Miguel does it with every meal."

LOBSTER Y COCONUT CEVICHE

Lobster has a natural sweetness, and this ceviche adds to that with coconut milk, white wine, and mangos. This dish is inspired by one in David Sterling's book *Yucatán*, but whereas he serves it warm, we chill it and serve it as a ceviche.

Serves 6 as an appetizer

6 small lobster tails (approximately 600g)
2 tablespoons canola oil
¼ white onion, minced
1 clove garlic, minced
2 medium-sized hatch chiles, charred, peeled, and seeds and veins removed
½ cup (typically around 30g) Recado Para Puchero (page 89)
½ cup (120mL) sweet white wine, such as Riesling
1 cup (240mL) fish stock
2 cups (480mL) coconut milk, unsweetened
1 teaspoon salt
¼ teaspoon ground white pepper
2 cups (300g) cherry tomatoes, sliced in half
1 mango, peeled, pitted, and diced
½ red onion, thinly sliced
2 cups (about 120g) croutons

1 To prepare the lobster tails, cut the shell underneath lengthwise to the fin. Use a paring knife to remove the digestive tract. Loosen the meat from the shell, but keep it attached by the fin.

2 In a deep saucepan with a lid, heat the oil over medium heat. Add the onion, garlic, and chiles, and cook until fragrant and translucent.

3 Add the Recado Para Puchero to the pan and mix well. Pour in the wine and bring it to a boil, then reduce to a simmer and cook for about 2 minutes.

4 Add the fish stock and coconut milk, return to a boil, and then reduce to a simmer. Cook 5 more minutes. Add salt and pepper.

5 Add the lobster tails, cover, and simmer 6 to 8 minutes. You are looking for a firm texture.

6 Remove the lobster tails from the liquid and reserve the liquid. Refrigerate both until well chilled, at least an hour.

7 Once the lobster has cooled, dice it or cut into slices.

8 Serve the ceviche in a bowl with some of the poaching liquid ladled over it, and tomatoes, mango, onions, and croutons to garnish.

TOSTADA DE CEVICHE NEGRO

This dramatic ceviche is tinted with the pitch-black Yucatecan seasoning paste Recado Negro. This recipe calls for mahi-mahi, but you can use a white fish of your choice.

Serves 4

¼ cup (30g) Recado Negro (page 88)
1½ teaspoon achiote paste
1 cup (240mL) orange juice
1 cup (240mL) lime juice
1 pound (450g) mahi-mahi (or other white fish), diced
1 teaspoon dried oregano
½ cup (120g) Pico de Gallo (page 57)
½ cup (80g) mango, diced small
½ cup (80g) pineapple, diced small (optional)
2 teaspoons salt
4 tostadas
1 cup (240mL) Crema de Aguacate (page 61)
Thinly sliced radish, for garnish
Chopped cilantro leaves, for garnish

1 Whisk together the Recado Negro, achiote, and juices in a bowl. Add the fish, oregano, Pico de Gallo, mango, pineapple, and salt, and use a rubber spatula to stir to combine. Refrigerate for 1 hour.

2 Spread ¼ cup of the Crema de Aguacate on each tostada. Top with the Ceviche Negro, and garnish with radish and cilantro.

Lobster y Coconut Ceviche

Tostada de Ceviche Negro

Mariachi Cielo Azul, made up of current and former University of Texas students, often strolls through Fonda San Miguel, entertaining weekend diners in the evenings.

TACOS DE COLIFLOR

Our plant-based take on Baja fish tacos comes in handy any night of the week. Instead of the typical breading method that uses eggs, we use Dijon mustard and almond milk to coat the cauliflower. A combination of rice flour, cornstarch, and tapioca starch imparts that nice crispy texture.

Serves 6

3 tablespoons avocado oil, plus additional for frying
1 head white cauliflower, cut into bite-sized florets
3 cups (720mL) unsweetened almond milk
3 tablespoons Dijon mustard
1 tablespoon chile powder
1½ teaspoons salt plus 1 teaspoon, divided
1½ cups (180g) rice flour
2 tablespoons (16g) tapioca flour/starch
¼ cup (30g) cornstarch
1½ tablespoons yeast
6 tablespoons granulated sugar
12 ounces (355mL) carbonated water
Corn tortillas, warmed, for serving
4 cups (320g) shredded cabbage
2 cups (480mL) Salsa de Poblano y Aguacate, cream omitted (page 61)
1 cup (240mL) Vegan Mayo Chipotle (page 65)

1 In a Dutch oven or heavy-bottomed pot, add oil to fill ⅓ of the way. We recommend avocado oil or canola oil. Over medium-low heat, bring the oil to 350°F.
2 In a large bowl add the cauliflower, almond milk, Dijon, chile powder, and 1½ teaspoon salt. Mix well to coat the cauliflower.
3 In large mixing bowl, combine the rice flour, tapioca, cornstarch, yeast, sugar, and 1 teaspoon salt. Whisk in 3 tablespoons oil, then slowly add the carbonated water, a little at a time, as you may not need all of the water. You want a thick pancake batter consistency.
4 Line a sheet pan with paper towels and set it next to your frying oil.
5 Use clean hands or a slotted spoon to add the marinated cauliflower in small batches to the bowl of batter. Mix lightly until the cauliflower is fully coated in the batter.
6 Slowly drop battered cauliflower into the heated oil. With a clean dry slotted spoon, move it around to help it fry evenly. Fry until golden brown, then remove with the slotted spoon onto the prepared sheet pan.
7 Repeat until all cauliflower is fried.
8 Keep these warm in a low temperature oven (200°F) until you are ready to build your tacos.
9 To serve, make tacos with warmed corn tortillas. Top the cauliflower with shredded cabbage, Salsa de Poblano y Aguacate, and Vegan Mayo Chipotle.

Patricia Quintana

The culinary world is where the late Patricia Quintana was most at ease. Beautiful and poised, she was known for her accomplishments as a chef (she trained in France, Switzerland, and Canada), a writer (with two dozen books to her credit), and a businesswoman (she owned a restaurant and a catering company, with cooking condiments that carry her name and label still available for purchase).

Her friendship with Tom Gilliland and the late Miguel Ravago led to impactful decisions that established Fonda San Miguel as a great destination restaurant. It was Patricia Quintana who suggested the elaborate and lavish Sunday Buffet. The successful event always sold out and was twice recreated in response to special invitations from the James Beard House in New York City.

Those who knew Patricia best say she was passionate about promoting the basics of Mexican gastronomy. She was known to turn to the true experts: local cooks and the elders who shared indigenous ingredients and techniques with her. The valuable information she elevated to a culinary art form earned her special recognition. Quintana was named Mexico's culinary ambassador to the world by the Mexican Office of Tourism and the Association of Restaurants of Mexico.

Tom Gilliland says, "Patricia's desire to share Mexico's cuisine with the world was a gift that we all hold dear to this day." He fondly remembers being among the guests she invited to her father's ranch and hacienda outside Mexico City. Other guests included the then-president of General Mills of Mexico, Texas-born celebrity chef and restaurateur Stephen Pyles, tequila aficionada Lucinda Hutson, and Southwestern chef and restaurateur Mark Miller.

Patricia Quintana died in November 2018. She was 72. Her legacy for successfully promoting true Mexican food continues with every meal served at Fonda San Miguel.

HUEVOS MOTULEÑOS

Huevos Motuleños, eggs stacked with tortillas and black beans, are often referred to as Mexican Eggs Benedict. The hearty breakfast dish is reputed to come from the pueblo of Motul, outside Mérida in the Yucatán Peninsula. Regardless of its origins, it is a delightful way to start the day and may be served as a full meal.

Serves 6

2 tablespoons vegetable oil or lard
12 corn tortillas
2 cups (480g) Frijoles Refritos (page 98)
12 eggs, poached or fried (see note)
Tomato Sauce
1 cup (4 ounces, 113g) shredded Monterey Jack cheese
⅓ pound (150g) ham, cut into small cubes
⅔ cup (100g) frozen green peas, thawed

Tomato Sauce

Makes 5 cups

7 large tomatoes, roasted and blistered
7 serrano chiles
1 clove garlic, chopped
3 tablespoons (45mL) vegetable oil
Half medium white onion, chopped
Sea salt and ground black pepper, to taste

1 To prepare the Tomato Sauce blend all ingredients in a blender.
2 In a heavy 12-inch deep-sided skillet or Dutch Oven, heat the oil over medium heat until it shimmers.
3 Fry each tortilla for about 10 seconds until soft and pliable using tongs to hold the edges. Drain on paper towels and keep warm.
4 On each of 6 warm plates, place a tortilla and spread with ⅓ cup Frijoles Refritos.
5 Place 2 cooked eggs on each tortilla and cover with a tortilla.
6 Spoon a generous serving of Tomato Sauce over each tortilla and sprinkle with shredded cheese, ham cubes, and peas.
7 Serve warm.

Note

An old restaurant trick for perfect poached eggs is to poach them in advance. Using a skimmer or slotted spoon, transfer them to a bucket of ice water. Right before serving, bring a small pot of salted water to a boil and dip the eggs in the boiling water just long enough to warm them through.

For fried eggs, fry them lightly, transfer to an oiled baking sheet, and hold in a warm oven for no longer than 10 to 15 minutes.

Pudin de Chocolate Amargo y Aguacate topped with Chocolate Crumble

Manjar Blanco de Coco with Honeycomb and Coconut Chips

PUDIN DE CHOCOLATE AMARGO Y AGUACATE

This pairing of chocolate and avocado, both ingredients of Mexico, has two benefits: It is much, much easier than the traditional method of making chocolate mousse, and it just happens to be vegan. Use Mexican chocolate in this dish!

Serves 6 to 8, depending on ramekin size

Water, to melt chocolate
1 ¼ cups (200g) dark chocolate (between 62% and 70%)
2 medium avocados, peeled and pitted
1 cup (240g) agave syrup
1 ¾ cups (128g) unsweetened cocoa powder
¾ cup (160g) oat milk, or plant-based milk of your preference
2 tablespoons pure vanilla extract
½ teaspoon fine salt

1 Bring a couple inches of water to a simmer in a saucepan. Set a heat-tolerant bowl in the saucepan to help regulate the heat. Melt the chocolate, stirring, in the bowl. Set aside to cool slightly.
2 Place all ingredients in a food processor. Blend until smooth and creamy, scraping down the sides of the bowl with a spatula as needed.
3 Spoon the mousse into ramekins and refrigerate, covered, for at least 3 hours or up to one day.
4 To serve, top with Chocolate Crumble.

Chocolate Crumble

Makes about 2 cups
1 cup (200g) sugar
1 cup (130g) all-purpose flour (may substitute gluten-free flour)
¾ cup (85g) cocoa powder
½ cup (115g) cold butter in small cubes

1 Place all ingredients in the bowl of a stand mixer. Using the paddle attachment, mix until combined and the butter is the size of small peas.
2 Pour onto a silpat-lined half sheet tray and bake at 325°F for approximately 15 minutes, tossing every 5 minutes.

MANJAR BLANCO DE COCO

This Yucatecan pudding is similar to the Middle Eastern dessert called mahalabiya. It is often a much plainer affair, flavored simply with vanilla, but pastry consultant Natalie Gazaui likes to flavor her version with coconut.

Serves 6

1 tablespoon sugar
¾ teaspoon salt
1 ½ teaspoon universal pectin
1 cup (250g) coconut cream, sweet
3 ¼ cups (800g) coconut puree
2 teaspoons coconut extract
Honeycomb
Coconut Chips

1 Combine the sugar, salt, and pectin in a small bowl; set aside.
2 Add the coconut cream and puree to a pot over medium heat. Whisk in the dry ingredients until dissolved. Once the mixture comes to a boil, lower the heat and simmer for 1 ½ minutes. Strain through a fine mesh strainer into a heat-tolerant container, add the coconut extract, and stir.
3 Pour into ramekins and chill for at least 2 hours, or up to overnight.
4 Garnish with Honeycomb and Coconut Chips, and serve.

Honeycomb

Makes about 4 cups

1 cup plus 1 tablespoon (210g) sugar
2 tablespoons honey
3 tablespoons water
2 teaspoons baking soda

1 In a saucepan, combine the sugar, honey, and water over medium-high heat and heat to between 305°F and 310°F. Remove from heat.
2 Stir in the baking soda.
3 Pour the liquid onto a parchment- or silpat-lined sheetpan and let cool completely.
4 Cut the candy into small pieces for garnish. Store in an airtight container.

Coconut Chips

Makes 2 ½ cups

1 ¼ cups (300mL) water
1 ½ cups (300g) sugar
2 tablespoons light corn syrup
2 ½ cups (200g) coconut flakes

1 Heat oven to 250°F.
2 In a medium saucepan, bring the water, sugar, and corn syrup to a boil over medium-high heat. Lower to medium-low, and once simmering, stir in the coconut. Cook for 1 minute and remove from heat. Let sit for 4 minutes.
3 Pour the coconut mixture through a mesh strainer and let strain really well. Spread the coconut on a parchment-lined sheet tray.
4 Cook until dried, with a little bit of color, about 45 minutes. The chips will finish drying a bit as they cool; stir periodically so they don't stick together. Use as garnish and store in an airtight container.

PANQUE DE ELOTE

This is a fairly common muffin-like treat found in bakeries in Mexico. The Fonda San Miguel version is made without flour, so it is gluten-free and very moist.

Makes 12 muffins

3 cups (400g, or about 4 ears-worth) fresh corn kernels
5 eggs
⅔ cup (125g) sugar
½ teaspoon kosher salt
1 teaspoon vanilla extract
½ cup (1 stick, or 125g) melted butter

1 Heat oven to 375°F. Grease a standard-sized 12-cup muffin tin, and set aside.
2 Add the corn, eggs, sugar, and salt to a blender. Blend into a puree.
3 Add the vanilla and melted butter, and pulse a couple times to combine.
4 Divide the batter evenly amongst the muffin divots. Bake 25 to 30 minutes, until the muffins spring back when touched. Let cool slightly and serve warm.

For easy removal—and an artistic presentation—line the muffin tins with fresh corn husks.

Bar lighting, created by Wes Lane of Evoke Designs, spotlights an eclectic collection of vintage cocktail shakers, seltzer bottles, and syphon bottles. Seats at the bar fill up early and fast, with thirsty patrons eager to engage in banter with bartenders and enjoy all the menu offers.

FONDA SAN MIGUEL
CUSTOMER FAVORITE

NUMERO UNO MARGARITA

This reposado margarita, served on the rocks, is a standard-bearer at Fonda San Miguel.

Makes 1 cocktail

⅜ ounce (11mL) Bauchant orange liqueur
⅝ ounce (18mL) simple syrup
1 ounce (30mL) freshly squeezed lime juice
2 ounces (60mL) Corazón Reposado

1 Rim a goblet or similarly shaped stemmed glass halfway with salt. Fill the glass with ice.

2 Shake all ingredients in a cocktail shaker full of ice for 30 seconds. Strain into the prepared glass and serve.

Brentley Weber

Brentley Weber knows a good investment is measured by more than numbers on a spreadsheet. As Prosperity Bank area president, he points to the generous returns received from having Fonda San Miguel as a client for 25 years.

But he doesn't ascribe monetary value to what Tom Gilliland and the late Miguel Ravago have freely given to him and his family. Instead, it's an abundance of hospitality and sincere fondness that extends to generations of the Weber family. One might call it true generational wealth.

"One of my fondest memories is of my son, Brady, sitting at the bar sipping a mocktail created especially for him!" says Brentley. Now a lanky teenager, Brady grew up in the restaurant. Brentley appreciates the familiarity with which his son and all the members of his family are treated: "It makes us feel like we are members of one big family."

Brentley and his wife, Joanna, have hosted many family gatherings at Fonda San Miguel over the years, including Christmas Eve and birthday celebrations. "The restaurant is a special place for me and my loved ones," says Brentley. The respected banker issues a strong financial forecast for the restaurant's future. "Once you experience the food, ambiance, and service, you realize why the restaurant is still here and going strong," he says. "Other restaurants are fortunate if they last a year to ten years, so to be in existence for fifty years truly says a lot about all the elements Tom holds to a high standard."

Remembering

MIGUEL RAVAGO

In 2008–2009, when we launched *Despierta Austin* (*Wake Up, Austin*), we wanted to produce a morning cooking segment. Of course, we knew Fonda San Miguel would be the perfect setting. We set up cameras near the tortilla-making area, and Miguel shared how to make Chile en Nogada, the traditional dish that celebrates Mexican Independence Day, 16 de Septiembre.

It was important to Miguel that we showcase authentic dishes and the high level of cuisine that Mexico offers, far beyond Texas and the Tex-Mex most people are familiar with.

Miguel was so kind, so welcoming. I can still see him wearing his chef's outfit. He was handsome and soft-spoken, and he had the ability to clearly articulate the cooking process. Combining the cuisine and food with the culture of Mexico was a story Miguel was born to tell, and Univision was honored to provide a media outlet for him.

Miguel told the story of the ingredients and colors and how each represents a color in the Mexican flag. That was before social media led to the creation of celebrity chefs. He was way before his time, and the camera loved him!

LUIS PATIÑO
President and CEO of Austin PBS
Former General Manager of Univision, Austin

Miguel brought beauty and delight to all, illuminating every room he entered. He was everyone's best friend. A consummate host, he took interest in the lives of all—friends and strangers, patrons and staff. He was always a true gentleman, even when he whispered ribald and irreverent thoughts (with a mischievous giggle!), so as not to offend others. Miguel was a trickster at heart, and his playful sense of humor found him pulling pranks whenever he could. In his presence, a warm abrazo was always close at hand.

LUCINDA HUTSON
Edible Austin, *October 2017*

Miguel was an extraordinarily kind person who was very close to his sister, Elizabeth "Betty" Saenz, and his mother, Amelia Velasquez Galbraith. He genuinely cared about everyone, from those who worked in the kitchen to customers and our special guests. It didn't matter who they were. He was so professional, and at the same time, he loved to have fun! Miguel also had unlimited sympathy for the pain and suffering of others.

JANICE HARRIS
Former FSM Office Manager

Memorable experiences I recall prior to the pandemic were the informal weekly gatherings at Fonda San Miguel. We began referring to them as "Fonda Friday," and those get-togethers sparked great conversations about what was going on in Austin, everything from art and performances to politics and other shared issues of concern. Miguel would prepare special platters, with samples of various dishes to be shared by all. Different people were invited or just happened to stop by. It was informal yet very intimate, just like being in your own home with the friends you most want to be with. And Miguel was the ultimate host who made everybody feel at home.

AMALIA RODRIGUEZ-MENDOZA
Community and Cultural Leader

I don't know any restaurant that is so involved in the community, politics, arts, and culture. Miguel will be remembered, along with Tom, for establishing deep roots in the community they loved so much. Although Miguel is no longer with us, he is remembered because he and Tom started from nothing and built it all themselves. There will never be another Miguel Ravago.

MATT WEISSLER
Companion of Diana Kennedy, Friend to All

Section Three

FULL BLOOM

AGUACHILE VEGANO

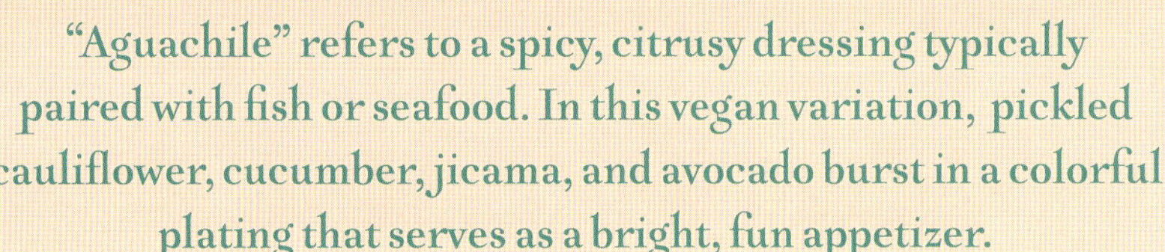

"Aguachile" refers to a spicy, citrusy dressing typically paired with fish or seafood. In this vegan variation, pickled cauliflower, cucumber, jicama, and avocado burst in a colorful plating that serves as a bright, fun appetizer.

Serves 6

2 cups (280g) each drained pickled purple and yellow Coliflor en Escabeche (page 94)
1 English cucumber, thinly sliced
½ jicama, peeled and thinly sliced
1 avocado, sliced
1 serrano, sliced
2 tablespoons thinly sliced red onion
Salt, to taste
Aguachile Verde

1 Arrange vegetables in an attractive manner on individual serving plates or a single large platter. Sprinkle with a bit of salt.
2 Spoon Aguachile Verde over the top and serve.

Aguachile Verde

¾ English cucumber, cut into medium-sized chunks
¼ cup (40g) roughly chopped white onion
1 tomatillo, husk discarded and cut in half
1 serrano, stem removed
¼ cup (60mL) fresh lime juice
¼ bunch cilantro
1 clove garlic
½ teaspoon kosher salt
1 cup (240mL) water

1 Combine all ingredients in a blender on high for 2 minutes to bring out the flavors and liquify. Strain through a fine mesh strainer into a bowl or pitcher.
2 Taste the liquid and adjust seasoning.
3 Keep cool until ready to use. This is best used the day it's made.

SIKIL PAK

This hummus-like pepita- and tomato-based dip hails from Yucatán. It's worth seeking out the tiny white pepita blanca, but regular roasted pumpkin seeds also work well.

Makes 2 cups

½ white onion
4 Roma tomatoes
½ habanero, stem removed
1 cup (140g) pepitas blancas
2 tablespoons bitter orange juice
5 sprigs cilantro, roughly chopped
Salt, to taste

1 Heat oven to 400°F. Wrap the onion in foil and roast it until softened, about 30 minutes.
2 In a dry comal or cast-iron pan, roast the tomatoes and habanero until charred in spots.
3 Pulse the onion, tomatoes, and habanero in a food processor. Then add the pepitas and bitter orange juice. The mixture should remain chunky.
4 Remove the salsa to a bowl, and fold in cilantro. Salt to taste.

TIRADITO MAYAN

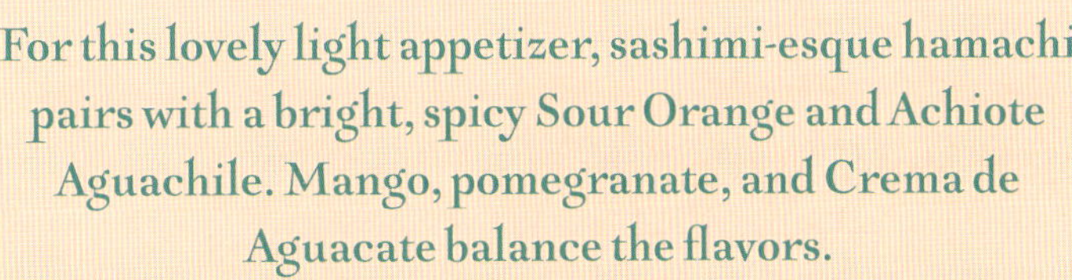
For this lovely light appetizer, sashimi-esque hamachi pairs with a bright, spicy Sour Orange and Achiote Aguachile. Mango, pomegranate, and Crema de Aguacate balance the flavors.

Serves 1

4 ounces (115 g) hamachi, thinly sliced
½ cup (120 mL) Sour Orange and Achiote Aguachile
Salt, to taste
¼ cup (40 g) mango, finely diced
¼ cup (60 mL) Crema de Aguacate (page 61)
2 tablespoons pomegranate kernels

1 Spoon Sour Orange and Achiote Aguachile onto a serving platter or bowl and lay out the hamachi in a shingle pattern on top. Season with salt.
2 Sprinkle with mango, dollops of Crema de Aguacate, and pomegranate kernals. Serve.

Sour Orange and Achiote Aguachile

Makes 1¼ cup

½ cup (120 mL) bitter orange juice
½ cup (120 mL) lime juice
1 teaspoon achiote paste
¼ to 1 whole habanero, depending on level of spice desired, stem and seeds removed
1 tablespoon rice vinegar
¼ teaspoon sugar
1 tablespoon Salsa Habenero (page 60)
Salt, to taste

1 In a blender mix all ingredients together.
2 Strain the liquid through a fine mesh strainer, and chill until ready to use.

Collection of vintage seltzer bottles (top shelf) and cocktail shakers (bottom shelf) from all over the world.

SUMMER SALAD

This is for those times when you've grilled your dinner but still have some heat on the coals to grill salad garnishes quickly. At the restaurant, we use a mix of whatever greens are growing in our garden and encourage you to do the same.

Serves 4 to 6

1 to 2 peaches, halved
1 cup diced watermelon
Kernels from 1 ear corn, cut off the cob
1 carrot, peeled and ribbon cut
8 ounces mixed greens, about 2 cups
Tajín Dressing
Salt, to taste
Pepper, to taste
¼ cup goat cheese crumbles
¼ cup Pepitas Dulces (page 95)

1 Heat grill to high. Place peaches cut-side down on grill and cook undisturbed until grill marks appear, 4 to 5 minutes. Flip peaches and grill until the skins are charred and the peaches are soft, 4 to 5 minutes more.
2 In a large bowl, toss to combine the watermelon, corn, carrots, and greens.
3 Dress generously but not excessively with Tajín Dressing, season with salt and pepper, and plate on a serving platter or individual plates.
4 Sprinkle goat cheese and Pepitas Dulceson top, and serve.

Tajín Dressing

Makes 1¼ cups

1 cup (240 mL) canola oil
½ teaspoon Tajín
Juice of ½ orange
Juice of ½ lime
Pinch salt
Pinch ground black pepper

1 Blend all ingredients on high speed for 30 seconds.

Crispy Oyster Tacos

CRISPY OYSTER TACOS

These fried oysters, inspired by a tostada dish at the famed Jeffrey's restaurant, in Austin, get their ethereal crispy coating from a seasoned combination of flours and cornstarch. Cornmeal works well on sturdy fish, but for delicate oysters, a lighter hand is needed. The tacos are dressed like many fish tacos: with cabbage, Chile Lime Mayo, and Pico de Gallo.

Makes 4 tacos

Oil for frying
3 cups (360g) all-purpose flour
1 ½ cups (180g) rice flour
¾ cup (96g) corn starch
1 ½ teaspoons chile de árbol powder
1 ½ teaspoons garlic powder
1 ½ teaspoons onion powder
3 teaspoons salt
2 teaspoons baking powder
2 cups shucked oysters

For Serving

12 6-inch corn tortillas
Chile Lime Mayo
2 cups (140g) shredded green cabbage
Pico de gallo, to garnish (page 57)
Lime wedges, for serving

1 In a heavy-bottomed pot, heat several inches of oil to 350°F.
2 In a mixing bowl, whisk together the dry ingredients to make the dredge.
3 Set up a sheet pan lined with paper towels next to the stove.
4 Coat the oysters in the dredge. Place oysters in a mesh strainer and tap to remove excess flour. Fry until golden brown (timing may vary, work in batches).
5 Heat the tortillas on a comal or skillet. Add a dollop of Chile Lime Mayo, place the oysters on the mayo, and top with cabbage and Pico de Gallo. Serve with a lime wedge on the side.

Chili Lime Mayo

Makes about 1½ cups (325mL)
Juice of 2 limes
¼ cup (30g) Recado Rojo (page 86)
1 cup (240 g) mayonnaise

1 Whisk all ingredients together to combine.

Nina and Frank Seely

Cappuccino Consultations

During the quiet hours before Fonda San Miguel opens, Tom Gilliland is likely found at his usual table in the dining room, poring over mail and magazines while sipping a cappuccino. It's a longstanding tradition he shares with consultants, and with consultants who have become friends.

Frank Seely is among the latter. The two men became acquainted in the late eighties, when Frank was busy building and remodeling various restaurants, including doing updates for Fonda San Miguel.

The cappuccino consultation sessions continued long after construction was completed. "Over the years, Tom and Frank met weekly for cappuccinos to talk about trends and issues," says Nina, Frank's wife. "They created a friendship that is very special to each of them. People often commented they should have their own radio program to share their thoughts on local and world views."

Frank introduced Nina to Tom and Fonda San Miguel when they started dating, in the early nineties. She recalls, "We didn't know at the time that we would weave a beautiful and eloquent friendship and bond that has been so meaningful to each of us over three decades."

The Seelys recall the first time they experienced the Plato de Miguel, which includes a bountiful portion of camarones, lollipop lambchops, quesadillas, tacos al pastor, and guacamole. "When Miguel brought it out," says Nina, "he said he wanted to have something that would give guests a lovely taste of the menu. We all loved it, and it's still a staple of the restaurant's offerings."

The cappuccino consultations continue as Tom and Frank discuss progress on Tzintzuntzan, the new venue next door for authentic Mexican almuerzo y desayuno. The two longtime friends are also talking about Fonda San Miguel's historic success and its preparations for its next fifty years.

Frank says Fonda San Miguel has stood the test of time because it is more than a restaurant. "Guests discover a restaurant like no other because of the art, the ambiance, the vibe, the architecture, and, of course, the menu and presentation," he says. "Families for generations have enjoyed the meaningful and personal experience that is Fonda San Miguel."

PESCADO ZARANDEADO

Gulf red snapper marinated in a rich adobo before grilling is an impressive dish that is actually quite simple to execute. This method of cooking fish comes from the state of Nayarit in western Mexico. Use a grill basket when it comes time to flip the delicate fish.

Serves 4

2 1½-pound skin-on red snappers, butterflied
Salt, to taste
Adobo Marinade
A few ½-inch wide slices white onion

1 Heat grill to high.
2 Season the fish generously with salt, then smother it with Adobo Marinade for up to 15 minutes.
3 Press pieces of onion onto both sides of the fish and place the fish in a grill basket.
4 Grill skin side-down first for about 3 minutes.
5 Carefully flip the fish over and grill for 2 additional minutes.

Adobo Marinade

Makes just under 1 cup

¼ cup (60 mL) vegetable oil, divided
8 chiles de árbol, stems removed
4 chiles guajillo, stems removed
1 clove garlic
¼ teaspoon whole cumin seeds
2 allspice berries
6 tablespoons water
¼ teaspoon Mexican oregano
¼ cup (60 g) mayonnaise

1 Heat 2 tablespoons oil in a pan over medium heat and sauté the chiles, garlic, cumin, and allspice until brilliant red, 2 to 3 minutes. Be careful not to burn them.
2 Blend chile mixture, water, and oregano in a blender until the spices have broken down and the mixture is smooth, at least 1 minute.
3 Heat the remaining 2 tablespoons vegetable oil in a sauté pan over medium heat (use previous sauté pan, no need to wash). Strain the chile puree through a mesh strainer into the pan.
4 Cook for about 30 seconds, stirring constantly. Remove from heat and let cool completely.
5 Whisk mayonnaise into the chile mixture.

PULPO A LA PARILLA

The sweet-fleshed Mayan octopus populates warm shallow waters off the coast of the Yucatán Peninsula. This recipe will work with colder-water octopus, as well, but the Mayan variety is worth seeking out, and all are exceptional when grilled.

Serves 6

1 Mayan octopus (typically found in Mexican grocery stores)
8 cups (1.9 L) water
½ cup (120 mL) bitter orange juice
1 ½ tablespoons store-bought pickling spice
½ teaspoon dried Mexican oregano
½ cup (120 mL) red wine vinegar
Salt, to taste
1 ½ teaspoons achiote
1 tablespoon orange juice
2 tablespoons Adobo de Guajillo, Pasillo, y Ancho (page 86)
Chili Lime Mayo (page 160)

1 Clean the octopus by rinsing it with water. If the octopus has not been trimmed, pinch and remove eyes with a paring knife or scissors. Spread the tentacles, flip the octopus over, locate the tough beak at the center of the octopus, and use a paring knife to remove it.
2 In a large pot, bring to boil the water, juice, pickling spice, oregano, vinegar, and plenty of salt.
3 Turn off the heat. Holding the octopus by the head, dip the tentacles into the poaching liquid 3 times. On the third dip, leave it in the liquid.
4 Turn the heat back on to medium-low and simmer for 40 minutes.
5 Use tongs to remove the octopus from the liquid and set aside to cool.
6 Once cool to the touch, remove the head and cut the octopus in half, so you have two 4-tentacle pieces.
7 In a small bowl, whisk the achiote and orange juice into a paste. Add the Adobo de Guajillo, Pasillo, y Ancho and whisk until smooth. Spread marinade all over the octopus, and marinate it in the refrigerator for one hour.
8 Prepare a hot grill. Grill the octopus on each side for 2 minutes. It should be charred in places.
9 Serve with Chili Lime Mayo.

SAN MIGUEL

Cordoniz con Pipián
de Semilla de Melon

CORDONIZ CON PIPIÁN DE SEMILLA DE MELON

Pipián is a sauce made with pumpkin seeds, but in this fresh summer version, we use both melon and melon seeds instead. It's lovely with grilled meats like quail, and you could also serve this sauce with chicken or turkey.

Serves 6

1 chile de árbol
1 cup (240mL) water, boiling
½ melon, peeled, diced, and seeds reserved
¼ cup (35 g) almonds
2 chipotle chiles en adobo
1 whole clove
1 cup (240 mL) chicken stock
1 cup (60 g) diced bolillo roll
2 tablespoons canola oil
Kosher salt, to taste
White pepper, to taste
6 quails
Recado Para Pollo (page 87, optional, or use kosher salt)

1 Add the chile de árbol to water. Remove pot from heat and let the chile steep to rehydrate.

2 In a dry skillet, sauté the melon seeds until nicely toasted, about 2 minutes. Set aside.

3 In the same skillet, toast the almonds briefly until fragrant, about 2 minutes.

4 Add the rehydrated chiles, chipotle, clove, chicken stock, and melon to a blender, and blend until smooth. Add the bread, melon seeds, and almonds, and blend until smooth.

5 Heat the oil over medium heat in the skillet until it shimmers. Add the pipián and cook it for 10 minutes. Season to taste with salt and pepper, and reserve warm.

6 Heat oven to 500°F.

7 Season the quails generously with Recado Para Pollo or kosher salt and pepper. Roast for 12 to 15 minutes, or until golden brown. Cut in half lengthwise and serve in a pool of sauce.

OMELETA DE HUITLACOCHE

This omelet combines the smoky, earthy flavor of huitlacoche with more standard omelet fillings like Pico de Gallo, corn, and cheese. Serve it with your favorite salsa.

Makes 1 omelette

2 eggs
Salt and pepper, to taste
2 tablespoons canola oil, divided
1 tablespoon diced onion
2 tablespoons Pico de Gallo (page 57)
2 tablespoons huitlacoche (see Sources, page 287)
2 tablespoons corn kernels
2 tablespoons shredded Muenster or Oaxacan cheese (optional)

1 Beat eggs vigorously with salt and pepper until foamy, and set aside.

2 In a skillet, heat 1 tablespoon oil over medium heat. Sauté the onion until softened, about 2 minutes, then add the Pico de Gallo, huitlacoche, and corn. Sauté until cooked through, about 3 minutes. Remove from heat.

3 Heat 1 tablespoon of oil in a small nonstick pan over low heat and pour in the eggs; let them set slightly, about 2 minutes, and add the cheese, if using. Dollop the huitlacoche filling on top of the cheese.

4 Fold the edges toward the center to cover the filling, and finish cooking for an omelette that is still creamy on the inside. Serve immediately.

Huitlacoche

Huitlacoche is a fungus that grows on ears of corn; in Mexico, it is a delicacy. Harvested and sold fresh, in season, most huitlacoche available in the U.S. is frozen or canned—at the restaurant, we prefer frozen. It has a truffle-like flavor and is often used as a filling for quesadillas. You can order it online and prepare it with scallops, as on page 171, or in an omelette.

CALLO DE HACHA CON HUITLACOCHE

Simple seared scallops make a fantastic accompaniment to a corn puree flavored with huitlacoche. Salsa Macha adds texture and heat.

Serves 4

12 U8 scallops
Kosher salt
Freshly ground black pepper
2 tablespoons vegetable oil
Huitlacoche Corn Puree
Salsa Macha (page 60), to taste

1 Pat the scallops very dry with a paper towel. Sprinkle generously with salt and pepper.
2 Bring a skillet or cast-iron pan to nearly smoking over very high heat.
3 Add the oil to the pan. Once it begins to shimmer, add the scallops, making enough room between them so they don't create steam.
4 Cook the scallops for 2 minutes without moving them.
5 Flip the scallops over, and cook for 1 minute.
6 Spoon the Huitlacoche Corn Puree onto 4 plates, and place 3 scallops on each. Top with Salsa Macha, to taste.

Huitlacoche Corn Puree

Makes 2½ cups

Water, boiling
1 chile de árbol, stem removed
2 tablespoons huitlacoche puree
1 tablespoon chopped white button mushroom
2 cups (320 g) corn kernels, cut off about 4 ears
2 cloves garlic
2 tablespoons chopped epazote
3 tablespoons canola oil
Salt, to taste

1 In a heat-tolerant bowl, pour boiling water over the chile and set aside to rehydrate, for about 20 minutes.
2 Add chile to a blender along with the huitlacoche, mushrooms, corn, garlic, and epazote. Add a little water if needed to help blend to a smooth puree.
3 Heat sauté pan over medium heat and add the oil. Add the puree, "fry" it for 5 minutes, and season with salt. Add water if necessary to maintain a puree consistency. Keep warm until ready to serve.

Coconut Lime Sorbet

Avocado Ice Cream

Strawberry Hibiscus Sorbet

Sesame Ice Cream with Raspberry Morita Swirl

COCONUT LIME SORBET

This fresh and bright sorbet benefits from a splash of liquor—a citrus liqueur, rum, or even vodka will help give it a luxuriously smooth texture.

Makes 2 quarts

Zest of 2 limes
⅓ cup (80mL) lime juice
½ cup (100g) sugar
½ cup (356mL) water
1 13.5-ounce (400mL) can coconut milk
1 13-ounce (385mL) can coconut cream
1 tablespoon liquor of choice

1 Add the lime zest and juice to a mixing bowl and let sit for 1 hour.
2 In a saucepan, bring sugar and water to a simmer. Stir until the sugar dissolves. Let cool.
3 Add the syrup, coconut milk, coconut cream, and liquor of choice to the mixing bowl and stir to combine. Freeze in an ice cream machine and proceed according to the manufacturer's instructions.
4 Store in an airtight container, and freeze for at least 4 hours before serving.

AVOCADO ICE CREAM

Avocado brings an unexpected creaminess to this ice cream, which is lovely served with chocolate and a pinch of cayenne pepper.

Makes 2 quarts

1 cup (240mL) heavy cream
1 ⅓ cups (320mL) whole milk
1 cup (200g) granulated sugar
1 ½ teaspoons kosher salt
10 large egg yolks
2 avocados
Juice from 1 lime
Shaved dark chocolate, ground chile de árbol, lime zest, and sea salt (or Tajín) for serving

1 In a medium saucepan, heat the cream, milk, sugar, and salt over medium heat, stirring occasionally, until the sugar dissolves. Keep warm.
2 Set up a large bowl of ice next to the stove, and set a smaller bowl that will fit the ice cream base inside it.
3 In a large saucepan, add the egg yolks. Whisking constantly, drizzle in warm milk mixture, then turn the burner to medium heat and continue whisking until it thickens slightly, about 4 minutes. The mixture should coat the back of a spoon.
4 Strain the ice cream base into the bowl set over the ice bath. Stir with a rubber spatula until completely cooled.
5 Add the ice cream base and the avocado to a blender and puree until smooth. Add the lime juice and pulse the blender to incorporate it.
6 Strain the ice cream base through a fine mesh strainer and refrigerate it for at least 4 hours, or overnight.
7 Churn the ice cream following the manufacturer's instructions. Store in an airtight container, and freeze for at least 4 hours before serving.

La Borda. Juan Torres.

Búho y tucán. Juan Vicente Rodríguez Bonachea.

Los visitantes. Leonora Carrington.

Photo of Drive-in, Monterrey, Mexico. Bob “Daddy-O” Wade.

Above: *Tras de ti*. Raphael Coronel.
Opposite top: *Pink Cakes*. Daniel Brennan.
Opposite bottom: *Still Life*. Daniel Brennan.

The Magician. Juan Torres.

STRAWBERRY HIBISCUS SORBET

Hibiscus gives everything a sassy pink tint, and this strawberry sorbet benefits from the tart flavor it adds, as well.

Makes 1 ½ quarts

2 pounds (900g) strawberries, trimmed
2 ½ cups (600mL) water, divided
1 ½ cups (45g) dried hibiscus
1 cup (300g) granulated sugar
Pinch of salt

1 Puree the strawberries in a blender, and strain through a fine mesh strainer to remove seeds.
2 In a small saucepan, bring 2 cups water to a simmer. Remove from heat, add the hibiscus, and steep for 1 hour. Strain to remove hibiscus blossoms.
3 In another small saucepan (or a bowl in the microwave), simmer ½ cup water and sugar until the sugar dissolves.
4 Combine all ingredients in a large mixing bowl.
5 Churn the sorbet in an ice cream machine according to manufacturer's instructions. Store in an airtight container, and freeze for at least 4 hours before serving.

Carol and Chris Adams

Charitable Couple

Throw darts while blindfolded at the names of Austin charities, and you'll hit more than one that Carol and Chris Adams have been involved with over the years.

In the late eighties, Carol organized fundraising events centered on Fonda San Miguel's Sunday Buffet. Proceeds benefitted the Sharir Dance Company, the ZACH Theater Actors' Fund, the Animal Trustees of Austin, Emancipet, and AIDS Services of Austin.

"No one has a bigger heart and a willingness to open their establishment to assist charitable organizations than Tom," says Carol. "And he has done so consistently for years. His generosity sets Fonda San Miguel apart from most other restaurants—and even most other businesses in Austin."

A philanthropic power couple, Carol and Chris have been together since 1980, when both were involved in Austin's intramural softball league. Chris was a fast-pitch softball player who coached a co-ed team—one of three teams Carol played for. In Austin's close-knit world of co-ed softball, Carol and Chris were among the only players who weren't coupled up.

At least not until the last game of their first season together, when Chris invited Carol out. It was a casual invitation she was eager to accept even though she had to break a standing date with another guy.

Since then, the Adamses have shared 43 years of marriage, two children, eight grandchildren, and too many charitable organizations to count—all of which have benefited from the generosity and stewardship of Carol and Chris. And Fonda San Miguel.

"Tom is recognized for his support of Austin's charitable community," says Carol. "Hundreds of thousands of dollars have been raised for so many nonprofit organizations—and that's just counting some that I've had the honor to lead."

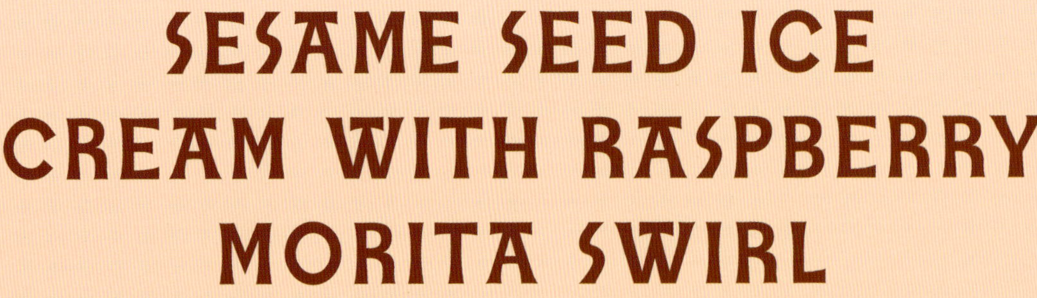

SESAME SEED ICE CREAM WITH RASPBERRY MORITA SWIRL

This is pastry consultant Natalie Gazaui's riff on a peanut butter and jelly ice cream, with sesame seeds standing in for the peanut butter. The morita chiles give it just a hint of smoke.

Makes 2 quarts

1 ½ cups (210g) sesame seeds, toasted
2 ½ cups (600mL) cream
4 cups (960mL) whole milk
2 cups (400g) granulated sugar
1 cup (200g) light brown sugar
2 tablespoons vanilla bean paste
(or the seeds from 2 vanilla beans)
½ cup (120g) tahini
24 large egg yolks
2 tablespoons kosher salt
About 1 cup (240mL) Raspberry Morita Swirl, to taste

1 Heat oven to 350°F.
2 Spread the sesame seeds on a sheet pan and toast until dark golden in color and very fragrant, about 3 minutes.
3 While seeds toast, bring the cream, milk, sugars, and vanilla to a simmer over low heat until the sugar has dissolved, about 7 minutes. Remove from heat.
4 Add tahini and toasted sesame seeds directly to the milk mixture from the oven. Steep for 1 hour.
5 Set up a large bowl of ice next to the stove, with a smaller bowl that will fit the ice cream base inside it. Set a fine mesh strainer in this bowl.
6 Heat the milk mixture in a pot just to a simmer.
7 In a large saucepan, add the egg yolks and salt. Whisking constantly, drizzle in the hot milk mixture, then turn the burner to medium heat and continue whisking constantly until it thickens slightly, about 4 minutes. The mixture should coat the back of a spoon.
8 Strain the ice cream base through a fine mesh strainer into the bowl over the ice bath. Stir with a rubber spatula until completely cooled.
9 Refrigerate the base for at least 4 hours, or overnight.
10 Churn the ice cream following the manufacturer's instructions. Right before the mixture is set, swirl in the Raspberry Morita Swirl. Do not over incorporate, so it remains a swirl. Store in an airtight container, and freeze for at least 4 hours before serving.

Raspberry Morita Swirl

Makes 1 pint

6 dried morita chiles, seeds and stems removed
1 8-ounce cone (225 g) piloncillo, roughly chopped or grated
1¼ cups (300mL) water
⅓ cup (80mL) apple cider vinegar
1½ cups (450g) raspberry jam

1 Heat a saucepan over medium heat and bring the chiles, piloncillo, water, and apple cider vinegar to a simmer, stirring occasionally, until the piloncillo dissolves, about 3 minutes
2 Add to a blender and blend until smooth.
3 Return the mixture to the saucepan and simmer over medium heat. Cook, stirring occasionally, until thickened into a glaze, about 5 minutes. The mixture should coat the back of a spoon.
4 Whisk in the raspberry jam until completely combined. Remove from heat and let cool completely before adding to the ice cream to create the swirl.

Head bartender, Barry Gamache

Elizabeth Avellan

A Family Affair

"Our first meal at Fonda San Miguel will always be a special memory," says Elizabeth Avellan. "It was a beautiful first meal gifted to us by thoughtful friends, prepared with love by Chef Miguel and uniquely presented to us by Tom. We were newlyweds, and in so many ways, it changed our lives!"

Elizabeth Avellan tells great stories. She also lives them and brings them to life on the big screen. She is the co-owner and vice president of Troublemaker Studios, the production company she founded 25 years ago with her former husband, the acclaimed filmmaker Robert Rodriguez.

The story of their memorable first meal began in 1988, when Elizabeth worked at the University of Texas at Austin in the office of the executive vice president and provost. There she met Robert, who worked as a clerk while taking film courses at the university.

"We were so poor, a familiar scenario for struggling creative students," Elizabeth says. "We couldn't afford to dine at Fonda, although we always wanted to. But friends and co-workers pitched in to give us a gift certificate as a wedding gift." The gift was orchestrated by the late Carla Steinbomer and her husband, Robert, an architect who provided input into the design of the restaurant's atrium.

"From the moment we stepped inside, from the first sip and the first bite, Robert and I fell in love with Fonda San Miguel, as so many patrons do," Elizabeth recalls.

The couple is credited as the director and producer of numerous successful film projects. Fonda San Miguel is a favorite place for Elizabeth and Robert to entertain A-list celebrities, including Academy Award–winning film director Guillermo del Toro, actors Josh Hartnett and Bruce Willis, and the cast of the Spy Kids franchise, including Antonio Banderas, Carla Gugino, Danny Trejo, and the late legendary Ricardo Montalban, for whom a chauffeur was arranged for travel to the restaurant every night of his stay in Austin.

The couple's off-screen credits include being the parents to five children, and although divorced, they remain good friends and professional colleagues. Over the years, both Robert and Elizabeth have returned to Fonda San Miguel to celebrate many special occasions. "Robert and I go there with our kids, grandchildren, siblings, parents and other loved ones. This restaurant is deeply ingrained in our lives, and Austin would not be the community it is without it."

Elizabeth says introducing guests to the food and atmosphere of Fonda San Miguel is like presenting each one with a gift. "Tom's mission of serving real interior Mexican food in an art museum setting is an extraordinary experience," she says. "I love to watch the faces of our friends as they melt in pure ecstasy, savoring the combination of flavors and sauces." The gift once presented to newlyweds grows more exquisite over time when shared with others.

Elizabeth Avellan and Robert Rodriguez in 1994.

Silver Coin Margarita

Tacos al Pastor

TACOS AL PASTOR

Rather than shaving meat from an inverse-bell-shaped trompo, as with gyros, try this recipe for juicy and well-seasoned nicely charred pork. Chiles, pineapple juice, and vinegar bring piquancy to this dish, which has Lebanese roots.

Serves 8 to 12

6 cloves garlic, minced
½ cup (120mL) neutral-tasting oil
1½ tablespoons oregano
1 teaspoon black pepper
4 whole cloves
7 guajillo chiles, deveined and torn into pieces
6 ounces (180mL) pineapple juice
⅓ cup (80mL) white vinegar
⅓ cup (80g) Recado Rojo (page 86), or achiote paste
1 teaspoon salt
3 pounds (1.3kg) pork butt, sliced into ⅛- to ¼-inch pieces (ask butcher to slice)
Corn tortillas
1 cup (165g) chopped pineapple
½ cup (75g) chopped white onion
½ cup (16g) chopped cilantro

1 For the marinade, heat a medium saucepan over medium heat and cook garlic in oil until fragrant, about 1 minute.

2 Add oregano, black pepper, and cloves and cook until fragrant, 1 minute or so. Add guajillo and continue to cook, stirring occasionally, for 3 to 4 minutes.

3 Add pineapple juice and vinegar, and simmer until guajillo pieces are soft.

4 Add Recado Rojo and cook for 1 minute, then blend until smooth and season with salt as desired.

5 Pour marinade over pork, cover, and refrigerate for 4 hours (or up to overnight).

6 Heat a grill to medium-high. Remove pork slices from marinade and wipe away excess. Grill 3 minutes per side, or until pork has a lightly charred crust.

7 Slice and serve in fresh corn tortillas garnished with pineapple, white onion, and cilantro.

SILVER COIN MARGARITA

You may want to vary the amount of lime juice, depending on the sweetness of your watermelon. Use the ripest, sweetest watermelon you can find, and your summer party guests will be very impressed and even cooler than when they first arrived.

Makes 1 cocktail

¼ ounce (7mL) lime juice
¼ ounce (7mL) lemon juice
¼ ounce (7mL) simple syrup
¾ ounce (22mL) Cointreau orange liqueur
1 ounce (30mL) Pueblo Viejo Blanco tequila
2 ounces (60mL) watermelon juice
1 small watermelon wedge, for garnish

1 Add all ingredients except the garnish to a cocktail shaker filled with ice and shake for 30 seconds.

2 Strain the cocktail into a martini or Nick and Nora glass. Garnish with the watermelon wedge.

Victoria Hentrich

Victoria Hentrich (left) calls herself one of Fonda San Miguel's biggest fans. She was an early customer, and she began organizing events at Fonda San Miguel on behalf of her clients, including a couple who invited guests to an engagement party and then surprised everyone by staging the actual wedding.

Victoria's career highlights include organizing two major events: the 40th and 45th anniversary parties of Fonda San Miguel, with 400 people in attendance at both and everyone, including the staff, in costumes.

"It's my responsibility to capture the mood and the moment, the art and the cuisine," she says. And her reward is witnessing the joy that events at Fonda San Miguel bring to her clients: "Brides are amazed at the opportunity to hold their wedding receptions there. It is like a dream come true."

Gray Hawn

For more than four decades, photographer Gray Hawn has earned worldwide acclaim for "capturing the moment." So it's no surprise Fonda San Miguel's unique ambiance has served as a backdrop for many of her professional photo sessions, whatever the occasion may be. "One of my fondest memories is of taking photos during the restaurant's 40th anniversary party," says Gray. "Just imagine larger-than-life costumed characters sauntering through a setting that is as familiar to you as your own home."

Fonda owners Tom and Miguel attended Gray's exhibit entitled "Romancing Mexico," and she says she is honored that her piece "Under the Bridge," featuring mariachi musicians resting between performances, continues to be on display at the restaurant.

Gray adds that two years ago, Tom hosted a book signing event for her daughter, Joy Saxton, and her children's book *Joy Goes to Mexico*. "Tom has been a wonderful friend to me and my family and has such an eye for art and creativity," Gray says, "and I think he is absolutely brilliant."

Amalia, Matt Weissler, and Diana Kennedy

Amalia Rodriguez-Mendoza

Mi Casa

"The first time I walked into that place I felt at home," says beloved community leader Amalia Rodriguez-Mendoza. "I loved the colors, the ambiance, and, of course, the food. It is a combination that fills my heart. It's where I belong."

The restaurant continues to feel like home to Amalia, especially now that her favorite dishes are on the De la Tierra section of the menu, which features plant-based "from the land" recipes introduced in 2022. "De la Tierra offers the vegetation, spices, and cooking techniques indigenous to Mexico that combine to create delicious, often healthier options," she says. "It's perfecto."

Feeling right at home at Fonda San Miguel, Amalia encourages others to join her. She promises first-time customers will leave feeling more than simply satisfied by a good meal. "Instead, they'll take with them a greater appreciation of the food's authenticity and for all the cultural contributions of Mexico and its people. It's the best restaurant in Texas!"

Impromptu gatherings at Fonda San Miguel fill Amalia with enough memories to last a lifetime. On one occasion, Diana Kennedy, the foremost authority on Mexican cuisine, was there with Tom and others, while another nearby table was occupied by guests of Univision and its general manager, Luis Patiño. That party included an artist who was performing on *Premios*, a television awards show featuring Spanish-speaking celebrities. Winners are selected by online audience votes, and past participants have included Ricky Martin, Shakira, Enrique Iglesias, Antonio Banderas, and Pit Bull.

"At yet another table was film director Robert Rodriguez and his guests," says Amalia. "Soon cross conversations between the different groups turned into a spontaneous party, with all the tables dining as one large group. Robert met Diana Kennedy, and they hit it off and were soon talking about his various film projects, her latest recipes and cookbooks, and their shared love of Mexico. It was an evening to remember."

CEVICHE LAS BRISAS

This popular ceviche was inspired by one in a restaurant in Boca del Rio, in the coastal Mexican state of Veracruz. A simple recipe, it is a guaranteed hit at parties, served with tostada chips and ice-cold beer. If black drum or redfish isn't available, you can use red snapper or Spanish mackerel.

Serves 6

1 pound (450g) skinned black drum or redfish filets, cut into ½-inch cubes
Juice of 8 large limes (about ½ cup)
4 to 5 pickled jalapeños, drained and chopped (use fewer for a milder dish)
2 medium tomatoes, seeded and chopped
¼ cup (60mL) olive oil
½ teaspoon dried Mexican oregano
½ teaspoon salt
½ teaspoon ground black pepper
Leaf lettuce for lining dish
Avocado slices
Lime wedges

1. Place fish cubes in a nonreactive bowl and pour lime juice over them; toss to coat well.
2. Cover the bowl with plastic wrap and refrigerate for at least 5 hours or overnight.
3. Stir occasionally with a wooden spoon.
4. And jalapeños, tomatoes, oil, and seasonings.
5. Toss well and drain.
6. Serve chilled in a bowl or footed glass lined with lettuce leaves and garnished with avocado slices and lime wedges.

Ceviche Las Brisas

Pepino Picante Margarita

PEPINO PICANTE MARGARITA

This spicy-fresh tequila blanco cocktail is a welcome refreshment at the end of a stunning spring day in Austin.

Makes 1 cocktail

1 2 inch-long section of a seedless cucumber
Tajín, for the glass
1 ounce (30mL) cucumber juice
4 dashes fire bitters
½ ounce (15mL) simple syrup
¾ ounce (22mL) Cointreau orange liqueur
¾ ounce (22mL) lime juice
1 ½ ounces (45mL) Arette Blanco tequila
Cucumber slice, for garnish

1 Puree the cucumber in a blender at high speed and strain into a container through a fine mesh strainer.

2 Rim halfway a double old fashioned glass with Tajín and fill with ice.

3 In a shaker filled with ice, add cucumber juice, bitters, simple syrup, Cointreau, lime juice, and tequila, and shake for 30 seconds.

4 Strain the cocktail into the prepared glass. Garnish with cucumber and serve.

David Kurio

Beautiful yet inviting is how Fonda San Miguel is often described. It takes a special talent to create the perfect floral arrangements and decor to enhance the Fonda San Miguel ambiance. That special person is David Kurio of David Kurio Designs, one of the best-known event design and creative services companies in Austin.

"The first time I walked into Fonda San Miguel, I was impressed with the ambiance and art, the lighting, and the magical environment," David recalls. He has created unforgettable first impressions for an untold number of guests since joining the ranks of the restaurant's favored vendors forty years ago. "I've been fortunate to collaborate with Tom and his team on special occasions, private weddings, and dinners."

One of his favorite dining memories involves an evening when the food and decor were enhanced unexpectedly. "We were enjoying dinner when suddenly all the power went out!" he says. "Our dinner was interrupted by a blackout. But before you knew it, the restaurant was lit by candles and the impeccable service continued!"

The Fonda San Miguel bar is a thing of beauty, a work of art itself. Dramatically lit, it features anthropomorphic figurines by Sergio Bustamante and a collection of mugs by an unknown artist from Mérida, Mexico.

Section Four

HARVESTING

ENCHILADAS SUIZAS DE HONGOS

These enchiladas get swathed by a vegan suiza sauce, which is equal halves Salsa Verde de Mesa and Queso Vegano. A chopped mushroom, caulfilower, and walnut filling brings plenty of umami to the dish.

Serves 4

For the enchilada filling

½ pound (225g) white cauliflower, roughly chopped
½ pound (225g) crimini mushrooms, roughly chopped
½ cup (60g) toasted walnuts
1 tablespoon cumin
1 tablespoon chili powder
1 tablespoon dried roasted garlic powder (or granulated garlic)
¼ cup (60mL) plus ½ cup (120mL) canola oil, divided
2 tablespoons chopped fresh cilantro
Salt, to taste

For the vegan suiza

2 cups (480mL) Queso Vegano (page 65)
2 cups (480mL) Salsa Verde de Mesa (page 57)

10 to 12 corn tortillas

1 Place the cauliflower, mushrooms, and walnuts in a food processor and pulse until everything is chopped into rice-sized pieces.
2 Add the cumin, chili powder, and garlic to the mushroom mixture and stir to combine.
3 In a large pot or sauté pan, heat ¼ cup oil over medium-high heat. Sauté the mushroom mixture until all the liquid has cooked off and the vegetables release the oil, about 20 minutes. Remove from heat, add the cilantro, and season with salt.
4 To build the enchiladas, set up a sheet pan lined with paper towels next to the stove. Heat oven to 350°F.
5 Heat ½ cup oil on medium-high heat. Once the oil is hot, use tongs to dip each tortilla in the oil for about 30 seconds to soften, not to make them crispy like chips. Move the tortillas onto the sheet pan as you go.
6 Add a couple spoonfuls of the mushroom mixture down the center of each tortilla, and roll it around the filling. Carefully line the enchiladas, seam side down, in a 9- by 13-inch baking dish.
7 Combine the Queso Vegano and Salsa Verde de Mesa, and pour this vegan suiza over the top of the enchiladas, making sure to cover the tortillas completely.
8 Place the enchiladas in the oven and cook for 15 minutes. Serve leftover suiza sauce on the side.

Roberto Santibañez

Separating Authenticity from Tradition

A native of Mexico City, acclaimed chef and restaurateur Roberto Santibañez wasn't sure he wanted to live in the USA, but that's where he found himself in the late nineties. He was working in New York City, but he wasn't happy there. His partner, Marco, wanted to travel to Austin to celebrate his birthday, which brought the couple to town and Fonda San Miguel, to what would be a life-altering career crossroads. "Meeting Tom and soaking in the authentic Mexican culinary culture he created at Fonda San Miguel led to the most intense and wonderful time in my life," says Santibañez.

It didn't take long for Roberto to be offered the position of chef, and he quickly became a respected member of the Fonda family who provided valuable input into recipes that are considered timeless classics and are reflective of his guiding philosophy. "We needed to separate authenticity from tradition because there is no tradition without innovation," Roberto says. "What I learned from my mother, who was an anthropologist, is that traditions are ever evolving. Every time you make a dish, it evolves as you innovate even slightly. For example, it may be the use of a different pan, a change in a prep step, or the addition or subtraction of a particular spice. The innovation may be ever so slight, and it may be to accommodate a changing palate or to meet a dietary restriction. Yet the recipe is authentic nonetheless."

An award-winning chef who owns several restaurants in New York City aptly named Fonda, Roberto describes his own cooking as modern but authentic. He credits Tom for helping guide his success, saying, "I learned so much from Tom about making good food every day and always holding others to high scrutiny. I learned that you must eat and dine in your own restaurant to be able to correct the cooks, the staff, and others."

Roberto doesn't return to Fonda San Miguel as often as he would like, but when he does it evokes great comfort, as was the case in October 2023, when he and Marco returned to celebrate a milestone birthday.

"When I walked into the restaurant it was like walking into my own family home, or like my grandma's, and it still feels like home," he says. "You immediately draw a sense of comfort from the lights, the ambiance, the music and the way everyone makes you feel welcome." The importance of making everyone feel welcome is the most enjoyable lesson Roberto learned from his time at Fonda San Miguel. It's a valuable lesson entrenched in both the tradition and authenticity of Mexican hospitality.

ENCHILADAS DE PATO

This eclectic enchilada preparation was developed by Roberto Santibañez during his tenure as Fonda San Miguel's chef and was subsequently re-created by Chef Miguel Ravago. The current version served at the restaurant differs slightly, but we like the way these serape-like layers of tortilla provide a protective covering for the succulent duck breast.

Serves 4

2 to 4 tablespoons safflower oil
4 8-ounce duck breasts (900g total), skin left on
1 teaspoon sea salt
8 corn tortillas
¼ cup (60mL) vegetable oil
½ cup (120g) Frijoles Refritos (page 98)
2 large tomatoes, broiled, skinned, and chopped (optional)
Pasilla chiles, toasted and shredded
Cilantro sprigs for garnish

Cilantro-Poblano Sauce

Makes 3 to 3½ cups

5 poblano chiles, roasted, peeled, seeded, deveined, and chopped
1½ cups (360mL) Caldo de Pollo Básico (page 99)
¼ pound (115g) fresh spinach, blanched in boiling water and pressed to remove excess moisture (about ¼ cup spinach)
½ cup (20g) cilantro leaves, loosely packed
2 teaspoons coarse sea salt or to taste
1½ cups (360mL) heavy cream

1 Prepare the Cilantro-Poblano Sauce. In a blender, combine all sauce ingredients except the cream. Blend until very smooth. Transfer to a heavy 2-quart non-reactive saucepan and bring to a rolling boil. Whisk in the cream and return to a boil. Immediately remove from direct heat (if overcooked the sauce will turn dark green). Keep warm.

2 To prepare the duck breasts, heat the safflower oil in a heavy skillet over medium heat. Fry duck breasts, skin side down, for 3 minutes. Turn, sprinkle with salt, and fry 3 minutes for medium-rare. Remove from heat and drain on paper towels. Slice each breast in several diagonal slices. Keep hot.

3 To prepare the tortillas, heat the vegetable oil in a small skillet until it shimmers. Lightly fry each tortilla just until soft, about 15 seconds on each side. Transfer to a tray lined with paper towels.

4 To assemble, spread 1 tablespoon of Frijoles Refritos on each tortilla. Ladle a generous pool of warm Cilantro-Poblano Sauce on each of 4 dinner plates and place a tortilla, with beans facing up, in the pool of sauce. Arrange a fan of hot duck slices on top of the beans. Sprinkle with chopped tomatoes, if desired. Cover the meat with another tortilla, beans facing down. Ladle a generous portion of the warm Cilantro-Poblano Sauce over the entire stack. Decorate with shreds of pasilla chiles and garnish with fresh cilantro sprigs.

CREMA DE CALABAZA Y ANCHO SOUP

The warmth of ancho chiles brings a complexity to this autumnal squash soup, which just happens to be vegan. The Pepitas Dulces are lovely as a spicy-sweet garnish, but if you don't have time to make them, store-bought roasted and salted pumpkin seeds work as well.

Serves 8

1 medium butternut squash, peeled, seeded, and diced
4 cups (960mL) unsweetened oat milk
2 dried ancho chiles, seeds, stems, and veins removed
1 dried chile de árbol, seeds, stems, and veins removed
Salt, to taste
Pepitas Dulces (page 95), for garnish

1 In a medium pot, bring the squash, oat milk, and chiles to a boil. Reduce to a simmer and allow to cook until the squash is tender, 12 to 15 minutes. It's better to overcook than undercook it.

2 Move mixture to a blender and puree until smooth (or use an immersion blender). Salt to taste. If the soup is too thick, add a bit more oat milk to thin.

3 Serve hot, garnished with Pepitas Dulces.

Ancho Relleno

Chile en Nogada

Chile Relleno de Lentejas

CHILE RELLENO DE LENTEJAS

This vegan riff on a chile relleno is filled with a lentil picadillo. It gets its sweetness from plantain and its pizzazz from bright red Salsa de Jitomate.

Serves 6

6 chile poblanos
2 tablespoons avocado oil
1 tablespoon minced garlic
2 tablespoons finely diced white onion
2 tablespoons finely diced Roma tomato (about ½ tomato)
¼ cup (40g) finely diced plantain (about ¼ plantain)
½ cup (100g) cooked lentils
½ cup (100g) cooked pinto beans (follow the step 1 instructions for Frijoles Refritos on page 98 until tender, not mushy)
Salt, to taste
White pepper, to taste
2 tablespoons chopped epazote
2 tablespoons water
1 quart (960mL) Salsa de Jitomate (page 64)
Freshly chopped cilantro, for garnish

1 Toast the poblanos over an open flame until burnt and blistered on all sides. Place them in a heat-tolerant bowl and cover to allow them to steam for 15 minutes or until cool enough to handle.
2 For the filling, heat the oil in a pot over medium-high heat. Add the garlic and onions and sauté for 2 minutes to bring out the flavors. Add the tomatoes, plantains, lentils, and pinto beans. Season to taste with salt and pepper, then add the epazote. Stir well to incorporate all the ingredients. Add 2 tablespoons water to help cook the plantains. Once the water has cooked out, remove the pot from heat and let it cool to room temperature.
3 To clean the chiles, use a paper towel to gently remove the skin but do not split the meat of the chile. Slit the length of the chile with a knife to carefully remove the seeds from the inside.
4 In a saucepan, warm the Salsa de Jitomate.
5 Heat oven to 350°F.
6 Lay peppers slit-side up, and carefully spoon in the lentil mixture to fill up the poblanos entirely. Line up on a sheet pan sprayed with vegetable oil.
7 Bake the poblanos for 10 to 12 minutes, until warmed through (an internal thermometer should read 165°F).
8 Serve the poblanos with the Salsa de Jitomate and chopped cilantro.

Lentils

Makes just over 2 cups

1 cup (200g) dried brown lentils
½ white onion, skin removed
2 cloves garlic, smashed
6 cups (1.4L) water
Salt, to taste

1 Place all ingredients in a pot and simmer, uncovered, until the lentils are tender, about 20 minutes. Add water if too much of your cooking liquid simmers off.
2 Season to taste with salt, discard onion and garlic, and drain before using.

ANCHO RELLENO

One hallmark of Roberto Santibañez's years at Fonda San Miguel is the presentation of "off-menu" dinner specials. This unique chile relleno, with its distinctive light Picadillo de Pollo, was so popular that it became a regular menu item. Arroz Blanco or Frijoles Refritos—or both!—are super sides for this dish.

Serves 8

FONDA SAN MIGUEL 1975 2025 CLASSIC RECIPE

Picadillo de Pollo

½ cup (120mL) mild olive oil, divided
½ of a medium white onion, finely chopped (about 1 cup)
2 tablespoons minced garlic
2 pounds (900g) Roma tomatoes, finely diced (about 4 cups)
¼ teaspoon dried thyme
2 small bay leaves
¼ cup (40g) capers, well rinsed and drained
½ cup (75g) pitted Manzanilla olives, chopped
½ cup (80g) raisins
2 pounds (900g) finely chopped or coarsely ground chicken
1 teaspoon sea salt
½ cup (70g) slivered almonds
¼ cup (15g) firmly packed minced cilantro leaves
½ cup (30g) firmly packed minced parsley leaves
1 tablespoon minced mint leaves

Chiles

4 cups (960mL) water
4 ounces (115g) piloncillo, grated
½-inch piece of a Mexican cinnamon stick
⅔ cup (160mL) cider vinegar
½ teaspoon sea salt
8 large ancho chiles, slit open lengthwise, seeded and deveined

Cream Sauce for Anchos Rellenos

Makes 1 cup

2 cups (480mL) sour cream
½ cup (75g) minced white onion
½ cup (15g) firmly packed cilantro leaves, minced
½ teaspoon coarse sea salt

1 To prepare the Picadillo de Pollo, in a medium saucepan heat ¼ cup olive oil over medium heat and lightly fry the onion until translucent, 4 to 5 minutes.
2 Add garlic and cook for 1 minute.
3 Add tomatoes, thyme, and bay leaves, reduce heat to simmer, and cook for 15 minutes.
4 Add capers, olives, and raisins and cook 10 minutes, stirring often.
5 In a heavy 12-inch skillet or sauté pan, heat ¼ cup of oil over high heat until smoking.
6 Add the chicken and cook until the chicken is dry, stirring constantly.
7 Add salt and the hot tomato sauce, reduce heat, and simmer 5 minutes.
8 Stir in the almonds and fresh herbs, remove from heat and allow to cool.
9 To prepare the chiles combine water, piloncillo, cinnamon, vinegar, and salt in a medium nonreactive saucepan.
10 Bring to a boil, reduce heat, and simmer until piloncillo has dissolved, about 5 minutes.
11 Add the chiles, cover, remove from heat immediately, and set aside to soak for 8 minutes.
12 Carefully transfer the chiles one by one onto paper towels to drain.
13 Preheat oven to 350°F.
14 Lightly grease a 13-by-9-inch baking dish.
15 Stuff each chile with a portion of the cooled Picadillo de Pollo and arrange in the prepared baking dish.
16 Cover with foil and bake 15 to 20 minutes or until filling is heated through.
17 While the chiles are baking, prepare the Cream Sauce for Anchos Rellenos.
18 Combine sour cream and onion in a 2-quart nonreactive saucepan.
19 Boil for 8 minutes. Strain. Add cilantro and salt. Keep warm.
20 Remove baked chiles from oven and serve immediately in a pool of warm sauce.

CHILE EN NOGADA

Chile en Nogada, stuffed chile in walnut sauce, is conventionally eaten in Mexico during August, September, and October, the months when Mexicans celebrate Independence Day and, coincidentally, the months when freshly harvested walnuts and pomegranates are available in the markets. The dish represents the colors of the Mexican flag: green, white, and red. In Puebla, chile relleno are battered and fried before they are sauced, but at the restaurant we serve a batter-free version.

Serves 10

10 poblano chiles
2 tablespoons vegetable oil
1 pound (450g) ground pork
1 pound (450g) lean ground beef
1 teaspoon salt, divided
¼ to ½ teaspoon freshly ground black pepper, divided
1 white onion, diced
4 cloves garlic, minced
1 ½ cups (350g) tomato sauce
1 cinnamon stick
¼ cup (50g) dried pineapple
⅓ cup (50g) raisins
⅓ cup (70g) almonds, skinless and toasted
1 apple, peeled and diced
1 pear, peeled and diced
1 peach, peeled and diced
Walnut Sauce
½ cup (85g) chopped parsley
½ cup (25g) deep red pomegranate seeds

1 Char chiles until blackened, place in a paper or plastic bag, and allow to cool slightly so steam loosens the skin. Peel off charred skin and remove all seeds (keep it green as possible).
2 For the filling, heat oil in a heavy-bottomed pot over medium-high heat. Add the pork and beef, and season with salt and pepper. Stir meat as it cooks to break up large chunks until cooked through, about 15 minutes. Use slotted spoon to remove it from the pot and set aside. Reserve fat and juices in the pot for onion and garlic.
3 Add onion to the pot and cook over medium heat, stirring until translucent, about 5 minutes. Add garlic, and saute for 1 minute.
4 Add meat back into the pot, with the tomato sauce and cinnamon stick. Cook at medium low heat uncovered until nearly all liquid has evaporated, 20 to 25 minutes.
5 Add dried fruit and almonds, and cook for 5 minutes.
6 Add diced fruit, and stir gently to avoid creating a mushy texture. Cook for 7 minutes or until fruit softens.
7 Taste and add salt and pepper.
8 Stuff each chile with ½ cup filling, then plate with opening facing down.
9 Pour ¼ cup of Walnut Sauce over each stuffed chile, garnish with parsley and a scattering of pomegranate seeds, and serve warm or at room temperature.

Walnut Sauce

Makes 3 cups

1 ½ cups (~160g, approximately 72) walnuts, shelled, skinned (see note), and chopped
¾ cup (180ml) milk
1 slice inch-thick French bread, diced
3 ounces (85g) goat cheese
1 cup (240ml) Mexican crema (preferred) or sour cream
¼ cup (60ml) dry sherry
⅛ teaspoon cinnamon
1 tablespoon sugar
½ teaspoon salt

1 Blend walnuts and milk to the consistency of paste.
2 Add remaining ingredients, and blend until mixture is completely smooth and the consistency of heavy cream.

NOTE: To skin whole walnuts, place them in a bowl with ¼ teaspoon baking soda and boiling water to cover. After 7 to 10 minutes, brown outer skins will peel off easily.

Blame these special nuts for the limited availability of Chile en Nogada. They are available fresh only from August to October. Sweet, with a hint of vanilla, walnuts from Amecameca de Juárez are the key to this dish, and they are unlike any other walnut you've ever tried.

Photos from the early seventies show Miguel and his mother, Amelia Velásquez Galbraith, center, who lived in Phoenix, and Tom with his mother, Elizabeth Gilliland, who lived in Sidney, Nebraska. The women were proud of their sons and became close friends. The restaurant's fortieth anniversary cookbook is dedicated to both women.

RECADO NEGRO MEATBALLS

These Yucatecan meatballs are unusual for a few reasons. Seasoned with the striking black Recado Negro, they are studded with minced hard-boiled egg whites and stuffed with whole yolks. Briny olives and capers bring a little zip to the complex sauce.

Serves 4 to 6

½ red bell pepper, finely diced
½ red onion, finely diced
1 Roma tomato, seeds removed, finely diced
2 cloves garlic, minced
2 tablespoons vegetable oil
Salt, to taste
Freshly ground black pepper, to taste
½ pound (225g) ground pork
½ pound (225g) ground beef
2 cups (240g) Recado Negro (page 88), divided
2 tablespoons capers, drained and finely chopped
2 tablespoons green olives, drained and finely chopped
3 hard-boiled eggs, peeled, whites minced, yolk left whole
1 gallon (3.8L) water
2 sprigs mint
2 sprigs epazote
1 white onion, halved

1 Sauté vegetables in oil in a large skillet over medium heat until softened, 5 to 7 minutes. Season with salt and pepper. Remove from heat and set aside to cool.

2 In a bowl, combine the meats and 1 cup Recado Negro with clean hands until well incorporated. Mix in vegetables, capers, olives, and egg whites.

3 Flatten ¼ cup portion of meat in your hand. Add 1 egg yolk in the middle and wrap the meat patty around it. Repeat to complete all the yolks. With the leftover meat, make regular meatballs out of ¼ cup portions.

4 Bring water to a boil, and add the meatballs, mint, epazote, the onion halves, and the additional cup of Recado Negro. Bring back to a boil, reduce to a simmer, and cook until reduced by half, about 1 hour. Season to taste and serve warm.

Arnulfo Mendoza, one of Mexico's most renowned weavers and painters, created this tapestry, which features dyes made from insects and vegetables, interwoven with silk. It serves as a backdrop for an ofrenda, or offering, in observance of Día de los Muertos, celebrated on November 1 and 2. People display photos and favorite items to remember and show love for their deceased loved ones.

Fonda
San
Miguel

Left to right: Mary Herr Tally, Rusty Tally, Forrest Preece, Linda Ball and Peter Martino.

Linda Ball and Forrest Preece

Neighbors First, Friends Always

"Fonda San Miguel has always been a big part of our lives," Forrest Preece says as he fondly recalls how the restaurant fits into the busy life that he and his wife, Linda Ball, lead in Austin. A retired advertising executive, Forrest is known for the personalities column he has written for the *West Austin News* for nearly 25 years. The table turns as he shares some of his many favorite Fonda San Miguel memories.

"The restaurant opened in 1975, a few months before Linda and I started dating," Forrest says, "and for most of our marriage, we were conveniently living right around the corner. How lucky we are to have this magnificent establishment in our midst and to experience its growth and changes."

That's high praise considering the source. Forrest and Linda are recognized, respected, and loved wherever they go without the burden of fame other celebrities often carry. They also are generous patrons of the performing arts, literary arts, and health-related causes. Forrest describes himself as a food and wine connoisseur, and he and Linda are friends with all the local chefs, including Fonda San Miguel's late executive chef and co-founder, Miguel Ravago. They can usually be found enjoying their favorite menu items in the best restaurants in Austin and in other major cities.

"Meals, so many meals!" Forrest says, of dining at Fonda San Miguel. "One honored the special guest Alice Waters, the godmother of farm-to-table cuisine. Dinners with Diana Kennedy, the leading authority on interior Mexican cuisine, included her sharing her views on food and life. At one dinner we brought jazz royalty to the restaurant, including the road manager for the Count Basie Orchestra. She was so taken by the Angels on Horseback that she emailed a week later asking the name of the popular antojito."

Forrest says that every major city has a restaurant that is part of its civic character: "Fonda San Miguel fills that role in Austin, with flair and good taste."

Fonda San Miguel

MIEL
PUEBLA

TACOS ARABES

In the 1930s, large numbers of Lebanese immigrants began coming to Mexico, and their impact on the cuisine has been profound. These tacos take simple Middle Eastern–style flatbread and stuff them full of spiced meat and sauces influenced by both Mexican and Lebanese flavors.

Serves 8 to 10

1 ½ teaspoons dried oregano
½ teaspoon thyme
4 teaspoons black pepper
1 to 2 cloves garlic, charred
¾ cup (150g) labneh
⅓ cup (75mL) sour orange juice (Sevilla orange)
1 ½ cup (75g) parsley
2 to 4 (400g) white onions, roughly chopped
1 teaspoon salt
3 ⅓ pounds (1500g) pork butt, sliced into ⅛- to ¼-inch pieces (ask butcher to slice)
10 pan árabe, or pita bread, warmed
Chipotle Shatta Sauce
Jocoque
Lime wedges

1 For the marinade, blend oregano, thyme, black pepper, garlic, labneh, and sour orange juice until combined, then add parsley and onion and blend once more. Salt to taste.
2 Pour the marinade over the pork and marinate for 4 hours or overnight.
3 Prepare a hot grill and grill the pork until cooked through, about 145°F on each side.
4 Slice thinly and serve in warmed pan àrabe (pitas), with Chipotle Shatta Sauce, Jocoque, and a lime wedge.

Lithograph prints by Joél Reydon. Clockwise from top left: Maíz, Escanoles, Chiles, Huexolotl, La Yuka, El Camota.

Chipotle Shatta Sauce

Makes ½ cup thick paste

1 3.7-ounce (105g) can chipotles en adobo
4 to 5 cloves garlic, charred
¼ cup (60ml) apple cider vinegar
1 ½ teaspoons oregano
2 tablespoons grapeseed oil, divided
¼ cup (40g) piloncillo
½ teaspoon salt

1 Blend the chipotles en adobo, garlic, apple cider vinegar, oregano, and 1 tablespoon oil until smooth.
2 Saute the mixture in 1 tablespoon grapeseed oil over medium heat until thickened, 7 to 10 minutes.
3 Add piloncillo and stir over medium heat until the sauce is a thick paste with jammy texture, 3 to 5 minutes. Stir in salt to taste.

Jocoque

Makes about 2 cups

¼ cup (60mL) neutral-tasting oil
2 to 3 habanero chiles, charred
¾ cup (150g) labneh
¾ cup (180mL) Mexican crema
Zest and juice (about 1 tablespoon) of 1 lime
½ teaspoon salt

1 In a small saucepan, heat oil gently.
2 Wearing gloves, slice habaneros into a few pieces and add to saucepan. When oil just begins to bubble, remove from heat, set aside, and allow to steep and cool.
3 Blend remaining ingredients until smooth.
4 Strain cooled habanero oil, add 1 tablespoon to labneh mixture, and blend to combine.

How are my little babies?
Please don't get up!
Rawther
Indeed
It's in the book!
Bueno, bye
Indubitably!
Top o' the morning
Hello my darlings!

"Friends! Joy! Love!"

— Roi James

The artist (center) captured both Tom Gilliland and Miguel Ravago (shown) in portraits that hang in the restaurant's main dining room opposite one another.

HUEVOS ARABES

Similar to a shakshouka or rabo de mestizo, this breakfast dish can be served with crusty bread or corn tortillas for dunking.

Serves 4

1 tablespoon olive oil
1 medium white onion, finely chopped
1 whole clove garlic
1 14.5-ounce (411g) can Mexican-style stewed whole tomatoes (with onions and jalapeños)
¼ green bell pepper, seeds removed
1 tablespoon fresh lemon juice
2 teaspoons salt (or to taste), divided
8 large eggs
½ teaspoon ground allspice, plus extra to garnish
½ teaspoon ground pepper, plus extra to garnish
1 teaspoon chopped fresh chives
½ teaspoon aleppo pepper flakes
Corn tortillas or crusty bread for serving

1. Heat oven to 375°F.
2. Warm the olive oil in a large deep cast-iron skillet over medium heat. Add the onions and garlic, and sauté until the onions become translucent, 5 to 7 minutes.
3. Add tomatoes with their liquid, green pepper, lemon juice, and 1 ½ teaspoons salt. Simmer on medium heat for 10 to 15 minutes, or until slightly reduced. Break up the tomatoes with a wooden spoon or spatula while cooking.
4. Discard bell pepper and garlic. Salt to taste if necessary.
5. Crack eggs one at a time into the simmering tomato mixture, spacing them evenly over the sauce. Sprinkle with allspice, ½ teaspoon salt, and pepper.
6. Cover loosely with aluminum foil and transfer the skillet to the oven. Cook until the whites are set but yolks are slightly runny, 7 to 8 minutes. (Cook longer if you prefer hard-cooked yolks.)
7. Top with chives and pepper flakes. Serve with warmed corn tortillas or crusty bread.

Tamales de Chocolate

TAMALES DE CHOCOLATE

These chocolate tamales are a rich, warm treat for Christmastime—or, really, any time.

Makes 18 tamales

18 corn husks, presoaked in warm water to soften
1 pound (455g) Oaxacan chocolate (either canela or almond)
1 ¼ cups (300g) masa for tamales (see page 31, or store-bought)
⅓ cup (75g) unsalted butter, softened
¼ cup (60mL) half and half
⅓ cup (33g) cocoa powder
1 teaspoon vanilla extract
¼ teaspoon salt

1 To set up a double boiler, bring a couple inches of water to a simmer in a saucepan. Set a heat-tolerant bowl in the saucepan to help regulate the heat. Melt the chocolate, stirring, in the bowl.

2 Combine all ingredients in the bowl of a stand mixer fitted with the paddle attachment. Mix until well incorporated.

3 Spread 2 tablespoons of the chocolate masa onto each corn husk. Because the dough is thicker than traditional masa for tamales, it may be easier to place a scoop on the husk and shape the tamal as you fold. Follow the tamal-folding method on page 52.

5 Set up a tamale steamer (see page 42). Steam the tamales for 1 hour. Let them cool completely and reheat by steaming before serving.

A luncheon menu from the early 1980s featured, as a graphic statement, the custom tilework that lined the famed tortilla station of Fonda San Miguel.

MEZCAL OLD FASHIONED

It's a small thing, but swapping the typical whiskey for mezcal in an old fashioned produces an entirely different cocktail. Use this recipe to try different mezcals, whether from the deep list at Fonda San Miguel or in your home.

Makes 1 cocktail

3 dashes orange bitters
3 dashes mole bitters
¼ ounce (7mL) simple syrup
2 ½ ounces (75mL) Del Maguey Vida Classico mezcal
2 2-inch strips of orange peel, divided
1 Luxardo cherry

1. Stir the bitters, simple syrup, mezcal, and 1 orange peel with ice for 40 revolutions.
2. Strain over a large ice cube in a double old fashioned glass. Garnish with the orange peel and cherry.

Harvey Kronberg

Harvey Kronberg, left, with Mexican Consul General Pablo Marentes, lives and breathes Texas politics, and one place he knows he can always find stimulating political conversation—along with an excellent meal—is Fonda San Miguel.

"When I come in, talking politics with Tom is always on the menu," he says. "I know I'm going to enjoy an hour of talk followed by twenty minutes of eating."

Harvey came to Austin in 1968 for college, but he didn't discover Fonda San Miguel until he was a staff writer for the *Quorum Report*, a nonpartisan newsletter that focuses on Texas politics. In 1989, Harvey purchased the *Quorum Report*, when Texas was headed by Republican governor Bill Clements and Democratic lieutenant governor William Hobby, Jr. Harvey recalls that on any given night during the legislative session, he would see staff members and legislators entertaining guests at Fonda. "Most people in politics are the steak-and-potato types," he says. "For me personally, it was eye-opening to be introduced to my first interior Mexican food restaurant. Fonda San Miguel was unique at the time, and it quickly became, deservedly, iconic."

Harvey credits Tom with the restaurant's longevity and continued success. "When you think of iconic unique restaurants, few come to mind and even fewer remain," says Harvey. "Tom is there every night. Most owners allow restaurants to run themselves, but not Tom. He oversees every detail. There's nothing like it in Austin."

Harvey Kronberg and fellow politicos may not always see eye to eye, but they can leave political disagreements at the door to Fonda San Miguel and step inside for a memorable meal.

Pornografía, *by Mexican artist and rock musician José Fors Fierro, gazes from the wall of Fonda San Miguel, while some of the restaurant's most beloved patrons tuck in and enjoy one another's company.*

Section Five

CELEBRATING NEW BEGINNINGS

MOLOTES DE QUESILLO

These sweet cheese-stuffed plantain fritters make a fantastic cocktail snack. A number of sauces complement them nicely, but at the restaurant, they are served with spicy-sweet Mole Poblano, sour cream, and queso fresco.

Serves 4 to 6, as an appetizer

3 ripe plantains, peels on
2 tablespoons plus ¼ cup canola oil, divided
1 teaspoon salt
¼ cup (½ stick) unsalted butter, diced
1 tablespoon granulated sugar
8 ounces (225g) Quesillo or Oaxacan cheese, shredded
1 cup (120g) flour
Mole Poblano (page 83), warmed, for serving
Sour cream, for serving
Queso fresco, crumbled, for serving

1 Heat oven to 375°F.
2 Lay plantains on a cookie sheet, and drizzle with oil. Add salt so plantains are completely covered. Bake for 30 minutes, until dark and softened.
3 While the plantains are warm, peel and squash them in a bowl with butter and sugar. Mix well.
4 Cover plantain mixture with plastic wrap and allow to completely cool.
5 Oil a sheetpan. Flatten a 2-ounce ball of plantain mixture (about the size of a golf ball). Add 2 tablespoons or so of cheese in the center, then fold Molotes over to make football shapes and set aside on the sheetpan. Repeat until all the mixture is used.
6 Heat ¼ cup oil in a skillet or cast-iron pan over medium-low heat until it shimmers.
7 Place the flour in a shallow bowl. Roll the Molotes in the flour, and fry until golden on both sides, about 5 minutes. Use a slotted spoon to move Molotes to a plate lined with paper towels.
8 Serve with Mole Poblano, sour cream, and queso fresco.

SHORT RIBS WITH MOLE POBLANO

While mole is worthy of celebration all on its own, it is work to prepare and thus often saved for holidays and other big events. This makes a lovely centerpiece for any gathering, accompanied by roasted vegetables and tortillas. Transform this recipe into pork osso bucco by substituting pork shanks for the short ribs.

Serves 4 to 6, depending on size of short ribs

6 short ribs on the bone
½ cup (120g) Recado Rojo (page 86)
Salt, to taste
Pepper, to taste
1 white onion, roughly chopped
8 cloves garlic, crushed
3 Roma tomatoes, cut in half
½ cup (120mL) oil
2 tablespoons dried oregano
6 bay leaves
3 avocado leaves
2 12-ounce Mexican beers (355mL each), such as Negra Modelo
1 to 2 quarts (1 to 2L) beef stock, as needed to cover ribs
Mole Poblano (page 83)

1 Heat oven to 350°F.

2 Heavily season the beef with Recado Rojo and a generous sprinkling of salt and pepper, ensuring the meat is fully covered.

3 Line a Dutch oven or heavy-bottomed pot with a lid with the onion, garlic, and tomatoes.

4 Heat a large skillet on high heat and add the oil. Once oil is hot, sear the ribs on each side. Remove them to the Dutch oven.

5 Add oregano, leaves, and beers to the beef, and cover with the beef stock. Cover and cook in the oven for 1 ½ hours, or until the beef pulls away from the bone.

6 Serve with warm Mole Poblano.

POZOLE ROJO

Jalisco, Mexico, is famous for its red pozole, and former longtime Fonda chef Oscar Alvarez is famous for this version. The soup is both flavorful and filling, typically served with customizable garnishes.

Serves 6

3 pounds (1.3kg) pork butt, cut into 1-inch pieces
Salt, to taste
Pepper, to taste
2 tablespoons canola oil
1 white onion, diced
8 cloves garlic, minced
4 teaspoons dried oregano
2 bay leaves
4 cups (946mL) water
6 guajillo chiles, seeds removed
2 chiles de árbol
2 15-ounce cans white hominy (about 850g total), drained

1 Season the pork generously with salt and pepper. Heat the oil over medium heat in a large heavy-bottomed pot or Dutch oven. Working in batches, brown the meat all over. Remove and set aside.

2 In the same pot, sauté the onion and garlic until softened, about 3 minutes. Add the oregano and bay leaves.

3 Add the meat and water. Bring to a boil, reduce to a simmer, and cook uncovered for 30 minutes.

4 When the soup comes to a boil, pour 1 cup of the broth over the chiles in a heat-tolerant bowl. Let sit 10 to 15 minutes, then puree in a blender and add to the pot.

5 After the pork has simmered for 30 minutes, add the hominy and cook for 15 minutes.

6 Serve with garnishes, as desired.

Garnishes

The more the merrier for this dish. We serve it with shredded cabbage, oregano, diced white onion, sliced avocado, charred and sliced tostadas, sliced radish, cilantro, and lime wedges.

Gloria Mata Pennington

Gloria Mata Pennington (at left) faces a dilemma most Austinites would envy. The grande dame of the local Mexican American community has too many fond memories and has enjoyed too many favorite foods at Fonda San Miguel to choose a favorite.

Lucky for us, though, she shares one sweet and special memory.

"As we often did, my friend Amalia Rodriguez-Mendoza and I stopped by Fonda San Miguel to join Tom for a drink and light dinner," Gloria says. "As we were finishing, Chef Miguel Ravago asked if we were ready for dessert and explained he wanted us to taste a new item and share our opinion."

Everyone agreed, she recalls, and minutes later,

Miguel returned with beautifully presented folds of cajeta-filled pastry drizzled with caramel sauce and sprinkled with chopped pecans, with a dab of ice cream on the side. "We ate it and declared it scrumptious," Gloria says. "A huge grin came across Miguel's face and his eyes twinkled! What we tasted that night has become one of the iconic desserts of Fonda San Miguel: Crepas de Cajeta."

Sergio Bustamante

Mexican Artist and Sculptor

Walking through the doors of Fonda San Miguel leaves one feeling transported to a beautiful hacienda in Mexico. That is exactly the ambiance Tom hopes for, with a mix of exotic plants, hand-stenciled stucco walls, and a display of work by some of Mexico's best-known artists.

Chief among those is artist and sculptor Sergio Bustamante. His signature stylized faces are featured in sculptures and on fountains prominently placed throughout the restaurant. "Fonda is the home of splendid and fine works that represent the art and crafts of Mexico at a higher level," says Sergio. "Having my work inside Fonda San Miguel has been a privilege and an honor. It is special to know my work is endorsed and supported by Tom's good taste and his awareness of the contributions of artists from Mexico."

In 2019 art patrons eagerly welcomed Sergio as the guest of honor at that year's Catrina Gala, hosted by Mexic-Arte Museum. Sylvia Orozco, museum executive director, describes the excitement of having the artist present, saying, "Sergio is a master artist from Mexico, and he was very gracious, very generous. People were honored by his presence and valued the opportunity to hear from him and learn more about his work. He donated a major piece that was auctioned off, with the proceeds benefiting Mexic-Arte."

The guests felt privileged to dine with such an internationally recognized artist. And Sergio appreciates being part of the artistic landscape of Fonda San Miguel. "It is to be part of the friendly and generous heart of a wonderful being like Tom," he says.

Caras. Mario Mizrahi.

Oaxacan scene with Zapata. Felipe Morales.

Woman with Guitar. Artist unknown.

Husband and Wife and Child. Chas Barth.

Etching depicting wedding. Artist unknown.

Man exclaiming. José Fors

ENSALADA DE BETABEL

Beets grow in Texas during in the colder months, which coincides with South Texas's citrus season. We love using red beets, golden beets, and candy stripe beets in this salad to bring out not only their earthy-sweet flavors but also their diversity of color. We also use a variety of greens from the restaurant garden, depending on what's available.

Serves 8

2 pounds (900g) greens such as kale, chard, little gem lettuce, the greens from the beets, or a combination
½ cup (120mL) Hibiscus Vinaigrette
Salt, to taste
Freshly ground black pepper, to taste
2 cups (320g) diced Citrus Beets
2 whole fresh grapefruits, peeled and cut into segments
4 whole fresh oranges, peeled and cut into segments
½ cup (75g) Pepitas Dulces (page 95) or other candied nut

1 Toss the greens in the Hibiscus Vinaigrette and season generously with salt and pepper.
2 Plate the greens on individual serving plates or a serving platter.
3 Top with Citrus Beets, citrus, and Pepitas Dulces, and serve.

Hibiscus Vinaigrette

Makes about 3 cups

½ cup (100g) sugar
½ cup (120mL) water
¼ cup (10g) dried hibiscus flowers
Juice from 2 grapefruits
Juice from 4 oranges
¼ cup (60mL) red wine vinegar
½ cup (120mL) extra virgin olive oil
Salt, to taste

1 Combine the sugar and water in a small saucepan over medium heat. Bring to a boil and cook until the sugar dissolves. Add the hibiscus flowers, bring it back to a boil, then remove from heat and let steep for 5 minutes. Strain the syrup and let cool.
2 In a medium bowl, whisk in the citrus juices and vinegar. Slowly drizzle in the olive oil while whisking.
3 Season to taste. This may be stored in the refrigerator for up to one week.

Citrus Beets

Makes about 2 pounds

2 pounds (900g) red, golden, or candy stripe beets, greens removed and saved for salad mix, if desired
1 orange, quartered
½ cup (120mL) extra virgin olive oil
½ cup (120mL) red wine vinegar
2 tablespooons salt
2 tablespoons black peppercorns
Water, to cover

1 Heat oven to 350°F.
2 Wash the beets to remove any possible dirt.
3 In a Dutch oven or deep oven-safe pot with a lid, combine all ingredients.
4 Cover the pot and cook beets in the oven for 45 minutes, or until done, when easily pierced with a knife.
5 Use a slotted spoon to remove beets and place on a sheetpan to cool. Peel the beets by rubbing them with paper towels while warm; the peel should come off fairly easily.
6 Cut the beets into a large dice and refrigerate before using, for up to 5 days.

Server, Sergio Herrera

RULO DE SALMON

A unique dish with a stunning presentation, this salmon roll is a showstopper appetizer. Adobo-rubbed salmon is lightly charred, then cooled and wrapped in thin slices of cucumber. The garnishes are tropical fruits and cilantro oil.

Serves 6 as an appetizer

1 pound (450g) salmon
Salt, to taste
Freshly ground black pepper, to taste
½ cup (120mL) achiote diluted in 6 tablespoons water
½ cup (120mL) Adobo de Guajillo, Pasillo, y Ancho (page 86)
½ cup (120mL) lime juice
1 cup (240mL) orange juice
¼ cup simple syrup
3 English cucumbers, thinly sliced lengthwise and cut into 5-inch strips
1 mango, diced
¼ pineapple, diced
1 Fresno chile, thinly sliced
1 tablespoon Cilantro Oil

1 Season the salmon heavily with salt and pepper.
2 In a bowl, combine the achiote and Adobo de Guajillo, Pasillo, y Ancho. Use a brush to evenly apply sauce onto the salmon.
3 Use either a culinary blowtorch or a broiler to lightly char the top of the salmon, then allow to cool for 10 minutes. Cut the salmon into a small dice and place in a mixing bowl.
4 Combine juices and simple syrup in a bowl, pour over diced salmon, and mix well. Let marinate for 4 hours. Strain and reserve the marinade.
5 To assemble the Rulo, see pages 248 and 249.
6 To serve, garnish with mango, pineapple, chile, and drizzles of the marinade and Cilantro Oil.

Cilantro Oil

Makes 2 cups

1 bunch cilantro, blanched
2 cups (475mL) canola oil
1 tablespoon salt

1 To blanch the cilantro, bring a pot of salted water to a boil. Set up a bowl of ice water next to it. Boil the cilantro just until it achieves a bright green color, 30 to 45 seconds, and use a slotted spoon to submerge it in the ice bath.
2 Remove the cilantro from the ice water, squeeze as much water out as you can, and blot dry.
3 Blend all ingredients together for 2 minutes on high speed.
4 Strain through a fine mesh sieve lined with cheese cloth for a perfectly smooth oil. Store in the refrigerator for up to 2 days, or freeze.

1 Shingle 6 pieces of cucumber in a row, overlapping by about ½ inch on plastic wrap.

2 Use two spoons to squeeze and drain about ¼ cup of the filling.

3 Spread the filling along the close edge of the cucumbers.

4 Begin rolling the cucumber away from you.

5 Once the cucumber envelops the salmon, tuck it under the salmon and continue rolling.

6 If any of the salmon pieces fall out, tuck them back inside the roll.

7 Once the roll is complete, wrap it in plastic wrap.

8 Chill until ready to serve, then garnish according to the recipe.

Gluten Free Tart Shell, Large Round
Packing: 45 pcs/box
Net wt: 2.29 lb (1.04kg)
Batch no: 521152
Shelf life: 18 months
Best by: 02-08-2025
(MM/DD/YYYY)
Product N°:
THR55053CS
Vanilla Tart Shell, Large Round with Chocolate Coating
Packing: 45 pcs/box
Net wt: 2.89 lb (1.31 kg)
Batch no: 521313
Shelf life: 18 months
Best by: 06-06-2025
(MM/DD/YYYY)
VELVET
EVAPORATED MILK
VITAMIN D ADDED
Nestlé
La Lechera
Sweetened Condensed Milk
Sysco
Imperial
Cream of Tartar
ESPRESSO POWDER
BAKING SODA
Pistachio Crumble

CONCHAS

When pastry consultant Natalie Gazaui developed this recipe for the Mexican sweet bread, she thought twice. She knew she wanted a dough not quite as dry as typical conchas to create a treat you wouldn't necessarily need to dip in coffee, as is done traditionally. (Although these would be tasty with coffee too!) Here, she's provided a rich dough and four flavors of topping.

Makes about 24 conchas

7 ½ cups (900g) all-purpose flour
1 ¾ teaspoons salt
½ cup plus 2 tablespoons (125g) sugar
5 tablespoons yeast
5 eggs
1 cup plus 2 tablespoons (265g) milk
2 tablespoons vanilla extract
⅓ cup (75g) butter, softened
⅓ cup (75g) shortening, room temperature

Vanilla Topping

1 cup (110g) all-purpose flour
1 cup (110g) powdered sugar
Pinch of salt
½ cup (110g) unsalted butter, softened
1 ½ teaspoons vanilla extract

Strawberry Topping

⅓ cup (40g) Nesquik
1 ¼ cup (140g) all-purpose flour
1 cup (110g) powdered sugar
½ cup (110g) butter, softened
2 teaspoons strawberry extract

Chocolate Topping

¾ cup (155g) powdered sugar
¾ cup (90g) all-purpose flour
¼ cup (40g) cocoa powder
½ cup (1 stick, 125g) butter, soft
1 teaspoon vanilla extract

Corn Topping

1 cup (115g) all-purpose flour
⅓ cup (40g) powdered freeze-dried corn (available online)
½ cup (120g) powdered sugar
½ cup (1 stick, 125g) butter
2 teaspoons vanilla extract

1 In the bowl of a stand mixer fitted with the paddle attachment, combine dry ingredients on low speed. Alternate adding the eggs and milk, mixing on low until the wet ingredients are completely incorporated and scraping down the sides of the bowl after each addition. Add the vanilla and stir to combine.

2 Swap to the hook attachment. Knead the dough at medium speed until smooth and springy, 10 to 12 minutes.

3 Reduce the speed to low. A little at a time, add the butter and shortening, stirring between each addition until fully incorporated.

4 Turn the speed to medium and knead the dough again until smooth, 5 to 6 minutes.

5 Place dough in greased bowl and let rise, covered, in the warmest part of your kitchen, for 1 hour.

6 Punch the dough down and refrigerate, covered, until chilled, at least 2 hours but up to 2 days.

7 Divide the dough into 80g portions, about 20 Conchas. Roll into smooth balls and then gently stretch into stout discs about 5 inches across. Place on two sheet pans lined with parchment paper. Cover with plastic wrap so they don't dry out while you make toppings.

8 In a small mixing bowl, whisk together all ingredients except butter and extracts.

9 In the bowl of a stand mixer fitted with the paddle attachment, whisk the butter on medium speed until fluffy and lighter in color, about 4 minutes. Add half the flour mixture, stir on low speed until incorporated, scrape down the sides of the bowl, and then repeat with remaining flour mixture. Add topping extracts and stir until incorporated.

10 Roll 1 tablespoon of topping into a ball, then flatten it into a disc slightly smaller than a Concha. Press one on top of each Concha, flattening the dough slightly. Use a very sharp knife to score the topping into that famous shell design. Let rise until doubled, about 1 hour.

11 Heat oven to 350°F.

12 Bake the conchas for about 15 minutes. Let cool slightly, and eat warm or at room temperature.

Endy Teran Levin, left, and Ana Pool

Endy Teran Levin

An Evolving Role

When Endy arrived in Austin from Mexico, in 2008, she was a single mom, eager to meet people and find a job. She is grateful her friend Karen Frost introduced her to Tom Gilliland and Miguel Ravago. Endy describes meeting the well-known restaurant duo: "It was like being adopted! My twelve-year-old son, Mauricio, and I became immediate members of the Fonda family."

What started as a friendship developed into much more. "Miguel was from the Mexican state of Sonora, where my father was from," Endy says, "so it was like he and I spoke the same language." As for Tom, she says, "He suggested that I help organize special events in Mexico and here in Austin, so I assisted with the various guest chef gatherings and other celebrations."

A change in her personal life led to another shift in her relationship with Tom. As she began dating, Endy recalls, she felt more like a niece whose dates had to earn the approval of her Tio Thomas, as she affectionally calls him. "He would act like an older uncle and signal his opinion of my dates with a thumbs up or thumbs down," she says. After a chance meeting during a busy South by Southwest weekend, Endy fell in love with Brian Levin, who earned two thumbs up and much, much more. The couple married in 2012, with both Miguel and Tom in attendance.

Gradually Tom asked Endy and Brian to take on greater roles in his private life. Endy recalls Brian's early impression of Tom as "somewhere between being starstruck and trying to figure him out." She adds with a laugh, "Now they're buddies who talk about football, and they talk about me!"

The Levins also are Tom's travel companions, a role increasingly important as he faces occasional health challenges. The trio have traveled to Guadalajara, Mexico City, San Diego, and London. "Tom loves the best in everything and stops to admire things he finds beautiful," says Endy. "It can be anything from a car or a building to a pair of shoes."

Endy's importance in Tom's life continues to grow. She feels fortunate to get to know him so well and often sees the world from his viewpoint. "Tom is very sensitive, very emotional, which are both beautiful parts of him," she says. "Also his eye for art is so distinctive and it feeds his soul, and in turn, everything in the restaurant reflects that."

tzintzuntzan

Tzintzuntzan

Breakfast and Lunch Next Door

It seems impossible to contemplate topping a half-century of the successful operation of Fonda San Miguel. Fifty years of serving groundbreaking menu items, the legendary Sunday Buffet, and the restaurant's reputation as the first to introduce authentic Mexican food in Texas all remain unchallenged. Yet for Tom Gilliland, an unrealized dream has come true, the perfect way to begin your day, with authentic desayuno y almuerzo, breakfast and lunch.

Tzintzuntzan (pronounced zin-zoon-zan) serves "some familiar items," says Tom Gilliland, "but with the addition of a lot of new things that haven't been offered before in Austin." The idea is for Tzintzuntzan to be its own destination for foodies seeking out authentic Mexican breakfasts, with a panaderia, or bakery, and payoff for those craving unique flavors of ice cream.

To bring his dream to life, Gilliland hired Miró Rivera Architects, an internationally acclaimed firm well known in Austin. Tzintzuntzan, which means place of the hummingbirds, delivers a more contemporary feel, for which Miró Rivera designers are known, compared with Fonda San Miguel, with its hacienda style that transports one to Mexico. An open dining area and a courtyard connect the two venues and provide greater flexibility for hosting various sized social events year-round. Founding partner Juan Miró says, "A memorable space associated with a communal activity allows humans to feel connection. People need those spaces to come together."

Water features created by artist Sergio Bustamante enhance the airy and open feel of Tzintzuntzan, where breakfast and lunch patrons are seated for full service and a walk-up counter adds the right touch of convenience for patrons ordering to go. Spectacular and authentic, as Fonda San Miguel knows how to serve up best, Tzintzuntzan marks the beginning of the second fifty years.

From left: Endy Teran Levin, Tom Gilliland, David Cantu, Ken Jones, Juan Miró and Sergio Bustamante.

The path from Fonda San Miguel to Tzintzuntzan passes the gate to the garden, with the main entry of Tzintzuntzan in the background.

The patio's ample outdoor seating provides a serene view of the lovely garden and its water features, created by artist Sergio Bustamante.

Patrons can view the garden from inside the restaurant, and a convenient point-of-sale station allows easy takeout.

BLACK MOLE BISCUITS

These savory biscuits were something of a happy accident, says pastry consultant Natalie Gazaui. She had some leftover Mole Negro paste and biscuit dough, and the marriage of the two was destiny. Serve these with honey butter, made with Yucatecan honey, of course.

Makes about 10 biscuits

4 ½ cups (770g) self-rising flour
1 ½ tablespoons sugar
1 tablespoon salt
1 cup (2 sticks, or 225g) cold butter
2 cups (450g) full fat buttermilk, cold
1 cup (250g) Mole Negro paste (page 78)

1 In a mixing bowl, whisk together the flour, sugar, and salt.
2 Grate the butter into the flour and stir briefly to combine.
3 Add the buttermilk and gently toss the mixture with your fingertips until the buttermilk is evenly distributed. It should be tacky and shaggy.
4 See pages 262 and 263 for instructions for the dough.
5 Heat oven to 375°F.
6 Roll the dough out to a thickness of 1 inch, flour the top, and use a 3-inch biscuit cutter to cut the biscuits. Place them on a sheet tray and cover with plastic wrap. Refrigerate the biscuits 30 minutes. (At this point, you can freeze them if you like. Do not thaw before baking at same temperature and time.)
7 Bake for 20 to 25 minutes, or until the biscuits have risen and are golden brown.

1 Flour a work surface and pat the dough together to form a rectangle.

2 Cut the dough into 3 equal pieces.

3 Stack the dough pieces on top of each other.

4 Press the pieces into each other.

5 Use a rolling pin to roll out the dough to 1 inch thick.

6 Cut the dough into thirds again.

7 Stack the dough pieces on top of each other.

8 Roll the dough to 1 inch thick.

9 Spread a thin layer of mole on two of the pieces of dough.

10 Stack the mole-covered pieces of dough on top of each other.

11 End with the plain piece of dough on top.

12 Press the dough down.

13 Roll the dough to 1 inch thick.

14 Spread the mole on two of the pieces.

15 Stack the dough pieces, ending with the plain piece of dough on top.

16 Roll the dough to 1 inch thick.

17 Flour the top of the dough.

18 Use a 3-inch biscuit cutter to cut as many biscuits as you can. Cover the dough with plastic wrap, and refrigerate for 30 minutes.

Left to right are Consul General of Mexico Pablo Marentes, his wife, Patricia, Luis Patiño, and Tom Gilliland.

Luis Patiño

A Dear Friend Returns

Imagine leaving work in the evening, walking to your favorite restaurant, and being greeted by family members eager to serve you your favorite foods. That dream scenario is how Luis Patiño describes most days working as the general manager of the Univision television station in Austin, with Fonda San Miguel only a few blocks away.

"It was like my personal cafeteria!" he says. "I could walk across the street for comfort food served in a very welcoming environment." Just as conveniently, Luis took out-of-town executives to the 5-star restaurant, where the ambiance, service, and meals would always impress.

Luis is highly respected in the competitive world of broadcast television. He was a former vice president and general manager of both the San Antonio and Austin Univision stations before he moved to Los Angeles to assume the position of president and general manager of Univision Media Group. In 2022, he and his family moved back to Austin, where he is now the president and CEO of Austin PBS.

After 25 years with Univision in three markets, Luis says, it was a leap of faith to return to Austin, where so much had changed. But his return to Fonda San Miguel wiped all worries away. "At my first dinner, hosting Austin PBS board members, Tom brought in mariachis!" he says. "It felt like a homecoming, comforting to return to a familiar place. It confirmed a good decision at the right time for me, my family, and the community."

Austin PBS has become famous worldwide for original programming, including *Austin City Limits*. The station completed a yearlong celebration of its fiftieth year on the air, and Luis is excited about the future, including introducing more first-time guests to Fonda San Miguel. "It's a palace of elegance and sophistication," he says. "You feel you are being transported to another time in Mexico City or Guadalajara. It's a journey through time and space that you want to repeat often with others."

Tom's passion for the Mexican culture is evident everywhere you look and with every bite. "Fonda San Miguel is a cultural institution that makes us who we are: Mexican Americans," says Luis. "We are proud to take people there who might not understand or know true Mexican cuisine. The art, the authentic cuisine, the excellent customer service, the guayaberas worn by the staff, even the leather menu covers—it all provides a cultural experience at its finest."

Chilaquiles Verde and Roja

CHILAQUILES

Chilaquiles are all about texture: hitting the right balance of crispy chips soaked in sauce. If you have leftover chips, use them in place of the fresh tortillas here. Shredded chicken also makes a nice addition.

Serves 4

½ cup (120mL) canola oil
8 5-inch tortillas, cut into 1-inch squares
½ cup (75g) finely chopped white onions
Roja or Verde sauce
⅓ cup (40g) shredded Oaxacan cheese
4 fried eggs (optional)
Crema and roughly chopped cilantro, for serving

1 In a sauté pan, heat ½ cup of oil over medium heat until it shimmers. Fry the tortilla pieces, stirring occasionally so they don't stick to each other, until golden and crisp, about 3 minutes.
2 Use a slotted spoon to remove the tortillas from the oil onto a paper-towel lined plate. Drain the oil from the pan, except for 1 tablespoon.
3 Sauté the onions until translucent, about 3 minutes. Return the tortillas to the pan, then add the sauce, covering the chips as evenly as possible. Cover and cook about 3 minutes.
4 Sprinkle the cheese on top and add the egg, if using. Drizzle with crema and sprinkle with cilantro. Serve immediately.

Roja

Makes 1 cup

4 ancho chiles, seeds and stems removed
4 guajillo chiles, seeds and stems removed
1 medium Roma tomato
1¼ cups (296mL) water, divided
3 cloves garlic, roughly chopped
2 tablespoons canola oil
1 teaspoon dried Mexican oregano
Salt, to taste

1 In a heat-tolerant bowl, pour boiling water over the chiles and set aside to rehydrate for about 20 minutes.
2 In a dry cast-iron pan or skillet, cook the tomato over medium-high heat until softened, about 5 minutes.
3 Add the chiles and 1 cup water to a blender and blend until smooth. Strain the puree through a fine mesh strainer so you have a smooth paste.
4 Rinse the blender, then add ¼ cup water, tomato, and garlic, and puree until smooth.
5 Add the oil to a pan over medium heat until shimmering. "Fry" the tomato sauce for about 3 minutes, whisking, then add the chile paste and cook on medium high for 3 minutes. Add the oregano and salt to taste. The consistency of the sauce should lightly coat a spoon; thin it with a little water, if needed.

Verde

Makes 1 cup

12 ounces tomatillos, husked removed
4 serrano chiles, stems removed, seeds removed from 2 chiles
1 clove garlic, roughly chopped
1 tablespoon canola oil
Salt, to taste

1 In a small pot cover tomatillos with water and cook until just softened, 5 to 7 minutes.
2 Drain the tomatillos, reserving about ⅓ cup of the cooking water, and add it to a blender with serranos and garlic. Blend on high until smooth.
3 In a sauté pan, heat the oil and "fry" the sauce for about 5 minutes; it will reduce slightly. Season with salt.

Zapata, *by artist Daniel Brennan of San Miguel de Allende, is the first painting purchased for the restaurant, in 1975, and was hand-carried aboard a train for the journey to Texas. Bill Wittliff, the late screenwriter and author, admired it and made repeated entreaties to buy it, but the offers were politely declined.*

Fiestas
SUNDAY,
BRUNCH SPECIALTIES · COCKTAILS
BUY TICKETS
TRIBEZA

Corn Cookies with Strawberry Jam

CORN COOKIES

These easy-to-make Corn Cookies serve as a spectacular snack. They pair nicely with berry jams, particularly strawberry. You could also serve them with the Raspberry Morita Swirl on page 178.

Makes 24 cookies

2 cups plus 3 tablespoons (265g) all-purpose flour
¾ cup (105g) freeze-dried corn powder (find online)
¾ teaspoon baking powder
¼ teaspoon baking soda
1 ½ teaspoons salt
1 cup (215g, 2 sticks) unsalted butter, softened
1 ½ cups (305g) sugar
1 egg

1 Heat oven to 350°F.
2 In a mixing bowl, whisk together the dry ingredients. Set aside.
3 In the bowl of a stand mixer fitted with the paddle attachment or using a hand mixer, cream the butter and the sugar together until lighter in color and fluffy, 3 to 5 minutes.
4 Add half the flour mixture to the butter and stir until incorporated. Add the egg and stir until incorporated. Add remaining flour mixture and stir until incorporated. Scrape down the sides of the bowl with a spatula between each addition.
5 Line a sheet pan with parchment paper. Scoop 2 tablespoons of dough, flatten, and then crimp the edges with your fingers so cookies look like small tarts.
6 Bake for 15 minutes, or until the edges are light golden brown. Cool the cookies on the sheet pan for 5 minutes before transferring to a rack to cool completely before serving.

Strawberry Jam

Makes about 1 cup

¾ cups (150g) sugar
1 tablespoon green apple pectin, such as Pomona
2 tablespoons water
Just over 1 pound (500g) strawberries, trimmed and halved
Juice of 1 lemon

1 In a small bowl mix the sugar and pectin to combine.
2 In a heavy-bottomed pot, whisk together the water with the sugar mixture, and bring to a boil over medium-high heat. Once the sugar has dissolved, about 5 minutes, add the strawberries and the lemon juice. Mix to combine.
3 Let the jam come back to a boil, then lower the heat to medium-low. Stir frequently. As the jam thickens, lower the heat and stir more often to prevent it from sticking to the pot. The jam is ready when it slides off of a spoon in a sheet rather than dripping off.
4 Transfer to an airtight container and refrigerate.

Natalie Gazaui

Her Culinary Travels Continue

Traveling the world has greatly influenced Natalie Gazaui and her culinary creations. Raised in Uruguay in a home with Basque and Palestinian influences, she received culinary arts training in Italy. She's proud to contribute her personal Arab heritage to the fiftieth anniversary cookbook: "Finally Tacos Arabas are included as we focus on the many influences and contributions of diasporas in Mexico. We pay homage to the Lebanese community in Puebla and elsewhere."

Most recently, Natalie has traveled to Mexico to enhance her already extensive knowledge of desserts and pastries. Yet somehow her global journey returned her to Austin and Fonda San Miguel.

"Our lives intersected with publication of the thirtieth anniversary Fonda San Miguel cookbook," says Natalie of her relationship with Tom and Miguel. "At the time, I was a buyer at Borders bookstore and helped host a book signing, which led to a lifelong friendship with them."

When Natalie initially visited the restaurant, food didn't come first. "I was most intrigued by the artwork, because my mother is an artist and I grew up in a household filled with art," she says. "I wasn't yet paying attention to the meals and recipes. But that soon followed as I gained good friends in Tom and Miguel and we started hanging out at Fonda."

Cooking became her focus, and with the encouragement of everyone at the restaurant, Natalie embarked on a new career. She recalls, "I decided to attend culinary school, first in Austin and then in Italy. Before moving overseas, I put a placeholder on my time at Fonda and vowed to return. When I did, Tom invited me to come work for him."

Natalie worked the legendary Sunday Buffets, assigned to the center of the dining room, often alongside Miguel, to serve the patrons and explain various offerings. She perfected her ice cream and pastry skills before moving on to other Austin restaurants and eventually becoming a consultant. Natalie returned to Fonda in 2024 and immediately began providing input into the new adjacent venue, Tzintzuntzan, with its authentic Mexican desayuno y almuerzo (breakfast and lunch).

Natalie, who has since moved on from Fonda San Miguel, encourages world citizens to look beyond borders and politics and to remember that food brings people and cultures together. "Mexico has that aspect that few other countries have," she says. "Mexico is home to West Africans, the indigenous, the Aztec, the Mayans—these are the true authentic inhabitants who should and will be celebrated."

CAFÉ DE OLLA

A popular hot drink with its own ritual, Café de Olla is a traditional after-dinner drink. The dark, sweet brew is made with coffee, spices, and sugar boiled in a pot. The sugar is in the form of cones of piloncillo, Mexican brown sugar. When this beverage is served in the morning or to children, it is often diluted with steamed milk.

Serves 6

6 cups (720mL) water
1 3-inch Mexican cinnamon stick
2 whole cloves
3 ounces (85g) piloncillo, grated, or ¾ cup dark brown sugar
3 ounces (85g) dark roast regular ground coffee (about 6 tablespoons)

1 In a heavy 3-quart nonreactive saucepan, heat the water, cinnamon, cloves, and sugar over medium-high heat, stirring until sugar is dissolved.
2 Add the coffee and bring to a boil, reduce heat, and simmer 3 minutes.
3 Remove from heat, cover and allow to steep 3 to 5 minutes.
4 Strain through a fine sieve or coffee filter into warm mugs.

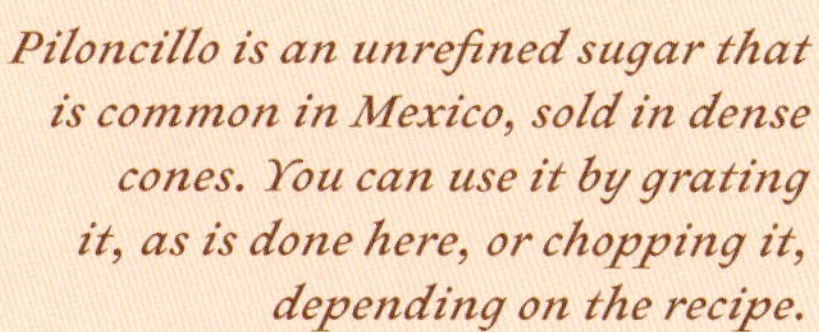

Piloncillo is an unrefined sugar that is common in Mexico, sold in dense cones. You can use it by grating it, as is done here, or chopping it, depending on the recipe.

Magnificent Building!

"When you step inside, it's like a holiday in Mexico, with all the beautiful art that speaks to you. It's something unexpected in Austin, Texas. And it's made even more memorable by the great food and excellent service."

— Victoria Hentrich, Event Planner

AGUAS FRESCAS

Aguas frescas are refreshing beverages served all over Mexico that are typically, but not always, made by blending fruit, water, lime, and sugar. One famous exception is horchata, which is a milky drink made from soaked rice and flavored with cinnamon.

Serves 6-8

Horchata de Arroz (Mexican Rice Agua Fresca)

1 cup (185g) long-grain white rice
1 cinnamon stick (about 2 inches)
4 cups (946mL) water, divided
½ cup (100g) granulated sugar (adjust to taste)
1 teaspoon pure vanilla extract
1 cup (240mL) whole milk (optional, for creamier horchata)
¼ teaspoon ground cinnamon

1 In a fine-mesh strainer, rinse the rice under cold water until the water runs clear.
2 Blend the rice, cinnamon stick, and 2 cups of water for about 1 minute. It doesn't need to be completely smooth—just broken down. Let the mixture soak in a covered bowl for at least 4 hours, or better yet, overnight. The longer it soaks, the richer the flavor.
3 After soaking, blend the mixture again with 2 cups of water until smooth. Strain it through a fine-mesh strainer or cheesecloth into a pitcher, pressing to extract all the liquid.
4 Stir in the sugar, vanilla, and milk. Taste it—this is where you adjust the sweetness to your liking.
5 Chill for at least 1 hour before serving. Serve over ice and garnish with a sprinkle of ground cinnamon.

Agua de Pepino (Cucumber Agua Fresca)

4 seedless cucumbers (about 6 cups, peeled and chopped)
4 cups (946mL) water, divided
½ cup (100g) granulated sugar (adjust to taste)
2 tablespoons fresh lime juice (about 1 lime)
Fresh mint leaves

1 Blend the cucumber pieces with 2 cups of water, sugar, and lime juice until perfectly smooth.
2 Strain the mixture through a fine-mesh strainer or cheesecloth into a pitcher. Press the pulp gently with the back of a spoon to get every last drop.
3 Add 2 cups of cold water to the pitcher and mix well. Taste it— adjust the sweetness or acidity with more sugar or lime juice.
4 Pour over ice and garnish with fresh mint.

Agua de Sandía (Watermelon Agua Fresca)

6 cups seedless watermelon, rind removed, cubed
4 cups (946mL) water, divided
2 tablespoons fresh lime juice (about 1 lime)
¼ cup (100g) granulated sugar (adjust to taste)
Lime wedges

1 Blend the watermelon cubes, 2 cups of water, lime juice, and sugar (if needed) until smooth.
2 Strain through a fine-mesh strainer into a pitcher. Press the pulp gently with the back of a spoon to get every last drop.
3 Add 2 cups of water to the pitcher. Taste and adjust the sweetness and acidity to your liking.
4 Serve over ice and garnish with lime wedges.

Chef's Notes

Horchata: Traditional horchata doesn't use milk, but adding it creates a luxurious creaminess. For a dairy-free option, almond or coconut milk works beautifully. Sugar is a personal choice; you can swap it for piloncillo or even agave syrup for a twist. Feeling festive? Add a splash of rum for an adult version.

Pepino: For a sugar-free version, honey or stevia is a great substitute. Add a few mint leaves to the blender for an herbal twist, or even a hint of jalapeño for a spicy kick. A splash of tequila or vodka transforms it into a party drink.

Sandía: If your watermelon is perfectly ripe, you might not need sugar at all. Blend in some mint leaves or a splash of coconut water for a tropical twist. A bit of vodka or tequila makes it perfect for summer fiestas.

Sylvia Orozco

Parallel Journeys

To know Sylvia Orozco is to know the importance of acknowledging, preserving, and sharing the culture and art of Mexico. It's the mission of Mexic-Arte Museum, which she and fellow artists founded as a nonprofit in 1985. What started in a small unassuming warehouse is now a recognized landmark, just blocks from the Texas state capitol on Congress Avenue. It remains the vibrant center for all aspects of Latino art in Texas and the Southwest.

Sylvia's vision for Mexic-Arte is closely entwined with the vision Tom Gilliland and the late Miguel Ravago had for Fonda San Miguel.

Sylvia arrived in Austin in 1975 to join her sister and attend art classes at the University of Texas. It was the same year Fonda San Miguel opened, with its unique offering of authentic Mexican food.

"I had lived in Mexico for five years and spent a lot of time in museums and in the homes of artists," she says. "I had been to the top of the pyramids and knew the goal and vision of museums. Fonda San Miguel had that vision too, how it looked and felt, the spirit of the restaurant, the quality of the art, and every serving of authentic food. I loved how it was put together. It was what I had experienced in Mexico. That was my vision for Mexi-Arte."

She began a quest to fill the void that existed in Austin and Texas, where no similar quality of museum existed with a focus on Mexican art. Her eagerness to share the beauty of Mexico's culture naturally led her to partner with Tom and Miguel. She recalls how the restaurant's ambiance was the perfect setting for potential donors to embrace her cultural cause: "We began inviting major celebrities, and we were fortunate to have the perfect place where people could begin to envision what a Mexican American museum could be."

She credits Fonda San Miguel with going above and beyond to attract financial backing. "Tom and Miguel had the resources to invite visiting chefs whose culinary, intellectual, and cultural vision was on point for Fonda San Miguel," she says. "Tom and Miguel knew exactly what they were doing. We were trying to achieve something so similar in concept, and we were on parallel journeys. They had the art of cuisine and had achieved excellence in that unique offering to others."

Hosting fundraising events for the future museum became a longstanding tradition. Sylvia's gratitude to Fonda San Miguel's abundance of hospitality over the years is echoed by others. "Our patrons, our artists, our staff, everyone is pleased," she says. "Even in 2020, when the pandemic halted all in-person engagements, including critical fundraising efforts, Tom stepped up and created a feast packaged to go. Patrons and donors stopped by to pick up their meals, and the museum program was successfully streamed live."

The pairing of the restaurant and museum is a beautiful and strong partnership that continues today. Tom Gilliland is recognized as an insightful connoisseur and curator of Mexican art, which is a distinct feature enjoyed by everyone who visits Fonda San Miguel. Tom and his many influential friends and guests continue to be major donors to Mexic-Arte Museum, and for that, Sylvia is immensely grateful. "Tom is a leader," she says, "and he is community and what he brings no one else does: the strong cultural pride of Mexico and its essence and beauty—not only in the restaurant and food but within the 'corazon' of Fonda San Miguel."

Sylvia is certain their parallel journeys are far from over. "My wish for Fonda San Miguel is for its continued prosperity," she says, "and that we continue to have a place to celebrate and elevate the art of Mexico and showcase the cultural contributions of Mexico and its people."

CARAJILLO

A simple but decadent espresso-based cocktail, the Carajillo is perfect alongside dessert. It gets its kick from Licor 43, a Spanish liqueur named for the 43 ingredients that give it a distinct flavor.

Makes 1 cocktail

1½ ounces (45mL) Licor 43
2 ounces (60g) espresso
3 coffee beans, to garnish

1 Add the Licor 43 and espresso to a cocktail shaker filled with ice and shake for 30 seconds.

2 Strain into a rocks glass filled with ice. Garnish with the coffee beans and serve.

Ana Pool

If the heart of a restaurant beats in its kitchen, then the brains are found with the office manager. At Fonda San Miguel, that is Ana Pool, who has been employed at the restaurant for 25 years. Her longstanding role began before she was born. Her mother, who made tortillas, met and fell in love with her father, who worked in the kitchen. Ana's parents provided her with a front-row seat to an exciting environment that unfolded before her eyes.

"It was an adventure and so interesting to grow up here, and I've enjoyed a full life as a result," she recalls. "It was almost surreal to be raised amid the public attention and publicity that a successful high-end restaurant attracts."

Ana knows an excellent dining experience is possible only because of the dedication and skills contributed by each employee. "Every person on the staff—the longtime chefs in the kitchen, who you will rarely see, or the person refilling your water and chips or the server and bartender who make sure your order is met or the hostess who manages to seat you at your favorite table—we all earn respect and deserve appreciation," she says.

Ana reveals that as a hostess, she practiced sorcery to maximize the restaurant's revenue. "I could see myself as a character in the movie *The Matrix*," she says, laughing, "with the power to look beyond limitations of the real world. I could see the restaurant's floorplan and tables and come up with solutions to maximize seating. The staff was amazed that every table was occupied! It was the Fonda San Miguel matrix—without bullets flying!" *¡Brava, Ana!*

SOURCES

Ingredient Sources

AGROPA AL LLC
Facebook: Agropa Escamoles and more
Instagram: @Agropa_llc
jose@agropallc.com
Here you will locate difficult-to-find Mexican ingredients, Mexican chiles, and chiles from around the world.

ÉPICES DE CRU
Website: spicetrekkers.com
Épices de Cru is a family-owned spice company based in Montreal whose goal is to provide the highest quality whole spices, respecting the traditions of producers and the needs of customers.

MUSHROOM MIKE
Website: mushroommikellc.com
Great source for huitlacoche!

RANCHO GORDO
Website: ranchogordo.com
This is a good source for heritage beans and hard-to-find Mexican ingredients like huauzontle and fried avocado leaves.

Ceramics

CERAMICASURO
Instagram: @ceramicasuro
C. 5 1006, Colón Industrial
44940 Guadalajara, Jal., Mexico
Sandra.castillo@ceramicasuro.com
52 33 36351298

GALERIA TALAVERA DE LA REYNA
Website: talaveradelareyna.com.mx
72810 Heroica, Puebla de Zarogoza, PUE. Mexico
52 22 22 25 41 82
Fonda San Miguel has a collection of their dinnerware that is presented for special dinners and events.

GORKY GONZALEZ
Website: gorkygonzalez.com
Calle Huerta, S. de Montenegro s/n, Pastita, 36090
Guanajuato, Gto., Mexico
52 800 346 8030

Galleries

CARAPAN
Miguel Hidalgo y Costilla
Oriente 305, Centro, 64000
Monterrey, N.L., Mexico
52 81 1911 9911
Well-curated handicraft gallery.

CASA DE OBISPO
C. Benito Juarez, San Angel,
Alvaro Obregon
01000 Ciudad de Mexcio, CDMX
52 55 5616 9079 (Sergio Mejia)
One of the most extensive handicrafts galleries in Mexico City near "Bazaar Sabado."

GALERIAS CORSICA
Guadalupe Sánchez 756 Centro,
Puerto Vallarta CP 48300
Email: corsicavallarta100@gmail.com
52 322 223 1821

LA MANO MAGICA
Website: lamanomagica.com
Gabriel Mendoza
galeriamanomagica@gmail.com
C. Macedonia Alcala 203
Ruta Independencia Centro,
Oaxaca de Juarez, Oax.
951-516-4275

SERGIO BUSTAMANTE GALERIA
Independencia Eje 238, Centro, 45500
San Pedro Tlaquepaque, Jal., Mexico
52 33 3639 5519
Email: tlaquepaque@sergiobustamante.com.mx

Furniture

CASA ARMIDA
Ancha de San Antonio 26,
Zona Centro, 37700
San Miguel de Allende, Gto., Mexico
Email: proyectos.ca@casa-armida.mx

MASSIVHOLZ
C. Bernardo de Balbuena 123, Ladrón de Guevara, Ladron De Guevara, 44600
Guadalajara, Jal., Mexico
52 33 1202 9037
Email:ventas@massivholz.com

MEXA
Av. Tepeyac 955, Col. Chapalita
Guadalajara, Jalisco
México. CP. 44500
33 9688 7698
Email: hello@mexadesign.com

Guayaberas

CAMASHA
Website: camasha.com
Avenida Ejercito Nacional Mexican 769 – 103 Granada 11520
Miguel Hidalgo, CD MX, Mexico
52 55 48 23 70 53

DOS CAROLINAS
Website: doscarolinas.com
There are no finer guayaberas in Mexico or the United States.
customerservice@doscarolinas.com
210-420-5587

SOBERANO GUAYABERAS
Facebook: Guayaberas Soberano
Oficial Av. Colón 506-j, Centro,
97000 Mérida, Yuc.
52 999 263 4478

DA
IGUEL
DA
N
30

INDEX

Note
Italic page numbers refer to illustrations.

Acknowledgments

We would like to thank Ruth Alegria, Kay Banning, Paul Bardagjy, Kevin Benz, Melissa Biggs, Kenny Braun, Olga Campos Benz, David Cantú, Chuck DeAses, Paula Forbes, Dana Frank, Barry Gamache, Kathie Garcia, Natalie Gazaui, Cindy Goldman, Carlos Gonzalez Gutierrez, Emily Gudeman, Humberto Hernandez-Haddad, Cory Leahy, Endy Levin, Pablo Marentes González, Ana Martinez, Tracey Maurer, Carlos Monroy, Jesus (Chucho) Moreno Hernandez, Rosalba Ojeda y Cardenas, Paulina Olague, Ana Pool, Sergio Remolina, Julie Savasky, Patricia Tejeda, Chuck Townsend, Brentley Weber, Melissa Whatley, and Blanca Zesati.

First Edition 2025

Published by Fonda San Miguel
2330 W N Loop Blvd, Austin, TX 78756

Photographs on page 25 by Jeff Wilson; page 87 by Mackenzie Smith Kelle; page 117 by Paulina Olague; page 255 by Julia Zeddies for *Tribeza*; page 258 by Wyatt McSpadden

Book Design and Production: Julie Savasky, Overstory
Recipe Consultant: Paula Forbes
Prepress: Professional Graphics, Inc.
Printing: Asia Pacific Offset
Printed in China

Library of Congress Control Number: 2025907766

ISBN: 978-1-4773-3328-0

Tradition, Passion, Hospitality

Passing the Molcajete

What a joy to have cofounded Fonda San Miguel with Miguel Ravago all those years ago. The experience has been a phenomenal part of my life. David Cantu will continue the legacy because now I am "passing the molcajete" to him. The future of Fonda San Miguel is assured. *¡Andale!*

Before I ever stepped through the doors, Fonda San Miguel was a place I dreamed about. It is more than a restaurant. It is a piece of Austin history and a reflection of Tom's lifelong love for Mexico and its remarkable culture.

Being asked to help carry that legacy forward is an honor I hold with humility. I'm grateful to Tom for trusting me with something so special.

The passing of the molcajete symbolizes this moment perfectly and reminds me what makes Fonda so special. It isn't just the food on the table. It's the way we blend tradition, passion, and hospitality into something people can feel the moment they walk in.

My promise is simple: to honor what Tom and Miguel built, stay true to the flavors and stories that brought Fonda to life, and make sure every guest feels the same warmth and joy that have made this place a part of so many lives.

Here's to honoring the past, embracing the future, and always serving from the heart.

TOM GILLILAND AND DAVID CANTU

FONDA
SAN MIGUEL
FONDA
SAN
MIGUEL
2330